You Couldn't Make It Up

You Couldn't Make It Up

Our adventures in small-town Provence

A.B. MONROE

Matador
Unit E2 Airfield Business Park,
Harrison Road, Market Harborough,
Leicestershire. LE16 7UL
Tel: 0116 2792299
Email: books@troubador.co.uk
Web: www.troubador.co.uk/matador
Twitter: @matadorbooks

ISBN 978 1803137 254

British Library Cataloguing in Publication Data.
A catalogue record for this book is available from the British Library.

Printed and bound in the UK by TJ Books Limited, Padstow, Cornwall
Typeset in 11pt Minion Pro by Troubador Publishing Ltd, Leicester, UK

Matador is an imprint of Troubador Publishing Ltd

To Marc and Beth, my fellow adventurers
and
To my beautiful father, who I lost along the way

NOTICE

This is not a guidebook to France, nor is it a book intended to tell you exactly how you will find the people of France. How you experience France can depend upon your age, your gender, your appearance and where you choose to live. We opted to rent a house in what French city dwellers can often refer to as *small-town* France to get back to basics, but with that decision came unexpected repercussions. I have written this book simply to share our experience because ultimately for the first two years we found ourselves uttering, "You couldn't make this up, this would never happen in Britain," which was said in a positive way, often addressing the lack of rules and restrictions that have caused (in the opinion of some) Britain to be classed as a nanny state. The last six years, though, we have been heard to say on almost a daily basis, "What the f***? What is wrong with the French?" Life can be very different in France.

Obviously, I have a legal obligation to protect the people we have met; therefore, all names and locations have been changed. One of the favoured conversations here in France by the French is how crazy they find their fellow compatriots, and we are not ones for disagreeing on this subject.

I should also add that when reading any dialogue spoken by a French person in this book, you should attempt to do so in your finest French accent, an episode of *Allo Allo!* should do the trick, and take into consideration that the French construct a sentence in English with the French thought process, which doesn't always make for good English grammar. Of course, English speakers can be guilty of the very same when speaking French (me included). Much of the dialogue noted in this book between French and English speakers has been written in a manner that gives both parties a fair chance at understanding each other.

The Author

Contents

"Yes, *grand'mere*" The clear brown eyes flickered and
blinked; he looked at once apprehensive and shifty.
His grandmother reflected that he knew nothing yet of
what his future was to be, he was in her hands, and for
a moment she felt the gratification of the power she had
never had over the silent, convent-bred girl, her son's wife.'
The World My Wilderness
Rose Macaulay (1881-1958)

'I have booked a trip on the *HMS Paris* and spending my time with a family I know in Cannes. I need to go to a place that makes me want to really go back home. A month with the French should do the trick.'

Violet Crawley, Dowager Countess of Grantham,
Downton Abbey

Introduction

Many people talk about living a better life, and some people succeed by finding a new life in their own country. Others, though, have a deep desire to live somewhere completely different. This was certainly the case with myself and with my husband, Marc. Finding home took us a lot longer than anticipated but thankfully France knocked on our door and upon reflection it was saying to us, "Come on, guys. Where are you?" We were not even considering France as an option and yet here we are, still here over 8 years later. We have faced enormous challenges, experienced extreme highs and lows and have had our fair share of family disagreements. We were extraordinarily naive when we landed in France and expected to be welcomed and to fit in quickly with French rural life. The truth is that the French can have their own unique and quirky ways, and fitting in can be tricky, and in our case, it left us asking ourselves, did we really want to?

Marc and I wanted to live somewhere where simple things mattered, where our daughter, Beth, could grow up without any unnecessary pressures. We wanted her to be in amongst children who were allowed to be children and who were not getting caught up with the competitiveness often driven by their parents who compared themselves to other parents, competing with giving their children designer clothes, the latest gadgets and ensuring that the Range Rover was polished ready for the school run.

Both coming from islands (Marc from New Zealand and me from the UK), we wanted to be part of something bigger, where we could get in our car and easily drive to another country, and that is exactly what we have done since arriving in France, with holidays to Spain, Italy, Switzerland, Austria, Croatia and Slovenia. Some weekends, we have taken the opportunity to drive over to Italy for pizza, using the chance to stock up on Italian wine. Why not! After all, Italy was just one and a half hours' drive away from where we lived. We craved fresh locally grown produce such as we had tasted on our trips to Italy and Greece, large, misshaped peppers and tomatoes that were sold for taste as opposed to appearance. Beautiful wine that we could buy directly from the vineyard without any snobbery attached to it. Long hot summers under a glorious blue sky allowing us to eat outside, and spending time by the pool, or swimming in the med, and last but not least, to live in a society that prioritised politeness. We wanted to have the opportunity to dress up and hit the town but also to dress casually and to chill out. Despite us arriving with the smallest budget, France has provided everything that we have asked for.

We have spoken to many people who have spent years talking and dreaming of moving to France, and they explain that the 'right time' never presented itself, and that is so true. A decision to swap country often means a leap of faith. The belief that everything will turn out all right in the end is our motto. It had to be. We had a very good lifestyle in the UK, but with the housing market crash in 2008 we lost just about everything. Our experience was humbling. We found ourselves in a rental house owing money, certainly not the situation that we planned when we envisaged moving to France. There was no 'right time', but we made the decision to do it anyway. For us, it was a massive leap of faith, plus we reasoned that we had nothing else to lose.

How we view the French now is incredibly different as to how we regarded them when we first arrived in this beautiful country. We trusted those who were polite, and shared our stories with those who appeared friendly. Why? Because that is how we behaved when we lived in our natural habitat, but this was an error on our part and a very easy trap to fall into in France. The French are very wary of the French, so take note.

Rose Macaulay's book *My World My Wilderness*, was set in Provence at the end of World War Two. If you haven't had the chance already to read this, I strongly recommend that you do so. I was lying on my sun lounger reading Rose's book by the pool in year six, a year the French family I write about were gearing up their antics. In her book Rose mentioned that she felt the war had left the French jealous and suspicious. I couldn't help but laugh, and this finally helped me to understand what we were up against.

There is of course the necessity of learning a new language. Some may feel that learning French is optional and to some degree, depending upon where you choose to set up home, it can be in France but only in very limited areas. In truth, speaking French is essential if you want to succeed in business and be treated seriously. When we first arrived, we made many mistakes, as we realised that it wasn't just our French that we needed to improve on but our etiquette too. We had become very used to getting straight to the point whilst conducting business and buying our shopping, and whilst we thought of ourselves as friendly people, we realised that we needed to spend more time interacting when entering a shop or buying groceries. The French expect you to ask them how they are, maybe to discuss the weather and generally to spend time with them. To conform, however, relies upon being able to speak and understand their language. The French can often speak very quickly and, added to that, they have their own slang which can change from region to region. We were under a considerable amount of stress when we arrived which did not help our ability to speak French, and we found ourselves mumbling and stumbling and in truth making complete arses of ourselves. Eight years on and whilst our French has improved greatly, it is only really Beth who could consider herself fluent. Marc and I continue to be corrected by the French on our grammar, and we continue to take it in the well-intended manner the advice is offered. Obviously, with most advice given but not requested, it can at times go in one ear and out the other, but we always nod politely.

Like many British people living in France, we had a scare when the whole Brexit malarkey kicked off. We had worked so hard to make France our home and had set up a successful business; it was not an option for us to return to the UK. Thankfully, despite the disappointing exit vote, life went on as normal for us and with a simple online application process, within three weeks we had received our residency visas. We were here to stay.

We will most likely always be outsiders living in France and that's the way we like it. We tried very hard to fit in when we first arrived and in so doing, we compromised our privacy and at times our happiness. We were not expecting to be welcomed into the family that we rented our house from or get caught up in their never-ending family disputes. We did not expect to be the centre of attention, be told how to live our lives and for our lives to be taken over by all the shenanigans that (may) look to encompass being part of a French tribal family. We were not expecting to meet people who became insanely jealous of our happiness and went to great lengths to create problems for us. It was exhausting. In the same respect, it was because of this family that we were able to rent our first house without showing any tax papers. This was the springboard that we sought and one that catapulted us later to a part of France that we had not envisaged staying in but a part that suited us all better as a family, one where money flowed freely and where happy positive people chose to live.

I tend now to be wary of the inquisitive French and I am inclined to reply to their questioning, "*Pardon, je ne comprends pas, je parle petit peu francais.*" (Sorry, I do not understand, I speak very little French.) This is often met with a look of despair and a few hand gestures as if to say why on earth do you guys keep coming over to our country if you cannot be bothered to learn our lingo? We continue to be polite but after our experience we remain wary.

In every country, I guess, there are people who go onto live a few streets down from where they were raised, continue to eat the same type of food they did when growing up, get together with a local girl or boy and have children without too much thought going into it, fall into a job that is not really of their choice or liking, are controlled by an overprotective mother, father or grandparent, feel they need a passport to leave their village and at the end of it all blame the government for their lack of achievement and happiness in life. Add to this, parents and grandparents who suspend the inheritance carrot in front of their children and grandchildren, which seems to give them control until the day they themselves die, and it could be said that this may well summarise some of the people who form part of *small-town* France. French city dwellers, in particular Parisians, can often be heard referring to country people as *péquenaud*s, *rustres ignorants* or *des bandes de paysans;* French terms that denote the type of people who in the eyes of city dwellers are deemed unsophisticated and unable to fit into any society that lies outside their small village. These are not terms that we ourselves use, but we do have a full understanding now of the type of people that are being referred to.

Beth once made a clever analogy of us living in France by comparing a rabbit leaving his rabbit kingdom to go and live amongst chickens. If he/she has the attitude that rabbits are far superior to chickens, he/she is not going to fit in. If he/she has the attitude of learning and adapting to the chicken kingdom, he/she has a far better chance of being accepted (very much our thought process). What though if the rabbit is a free thinker who adores his/her new surroundings but has unexpectedly found himself/herself surrounded by suspicious and jealous tribal chickens?

We had seven quite peculiar years living in Provence. I wish in truth that I had fabricated some of what I go onto recount in this book, because some of the people I have documented just about sent me over the edge. There is no doubt we were free-thinking rabbits living in amongst traditional chickens and quite frankly in the end we opted to leave, or as I prefer to imagine the event, we stuck our heads out of the kitchen window and yelled, '*TAXI!*'

We are now thankfully living amongst free-thinking rabbits; French, British, Dutch and Belgian to name but a few. Don't get me wrong; in the village where we opted to buy a house, during the renovation process we have had our share of inquisitive neighbours carrying on the French tradition of standing around observing and informing us what we can and cannot do, with frequent telephone calls to the local *mairie*, as they stand gossiping about us and most likely everyone else in the village. It would not be France if this did not occur, but unlike before, we quickly nip their chatter in the bud and keep conversations polite and weather based. We have realised that this French peculiarity is not confined to the small-town villages of Provence.

My grandmother used to say to us children, "Keep your nose clean and you will have a good life." If you choose to carry on and read the ridiculousness of the seven years we spent in Provence, I hope that you will see that we tried desperately (most of the time) to keep our noses clean, but the French, in all honesty, grabbed hold of us and beat us with sticks, nonetheless. A Frenchman once told me that you must be tough to live amongst the French or they will take advantage of kindness, which is often perceived as weakness. It is likely that this could well be one of the truest statements ever to be uttered from the lips of a Frenchman.

'To successfully live in France, one must learn the French art of suspicion, that of seduction and choose to live a private life avoiding contact with the green-eyed monsters who roam.'

The Author

One

It all started off very well...

10 December 2013. Five years of planning and finally we had arrived in Provence. In the glorious winter sunshine and on roads that we had become familiar with, we drove into one of our favourite French villages and put on our satellite navigation to allow us to navigate our way through the single-track tree-lined roads until finally we arrived at our accommodation. We had opted to rent a small house that was normally only rentable during the summer months, but the owners on this occasion had said that they would make an exception when I explained that we were coming out to France to live. Our house was located on the outskirts of the village backing onto fields lined with vines; it was an idyllic location. It was a modern single-storey house, south facing, with vibrant green shutters and a small covered-in terrace where was placed the typical sun-bleached and slightly peeling green plastic table with matching chairs. The garden was crowded with shrubs and flowers, with a large cherry tree taking pride of place in the centre of the lawn. To one side was parked our proprietor's campervan, and to the other side was a large parking area reserved for our use. Our terrace was private and perfectly

positioned to capture the daily sunshine, and we were desperate to unpack and set up lunch. Inside of the house, it was compact, a small hallway opening out onto a shared living/dining area, with a modern kitchen to the left, and further down the small hallway was to be found a shower room, toilet and two double bedrooms.

Our new temporary home was situated in a quaint little village thirty minutes from Aix-en-Provence, a village that we had stayed in on two previous occasions whilst on holiday. It was a practical base, being close to Aix-en-Provence and an easy jump onto the *autoroute* when it was time for Beth to start school.

Coming from Scotland, sunshine was a rare sight. Our daughter, Beth, recalls on our first morning me going out into the garden to take a photo of the sun. We had gotten used to suffocating clouds and drizzling misty rain that came at you no matter how you positioned your umbrella. In most cases your umbrella was blown inside out before you really had a chance to protect yourself from the elements. It was going to take time to get used to blue skies. One of the main reasons why we had selected this specific location was the documented 264 days of sunshine per year. It turned out that this was the motive for our new proprietors retiring down from Bordeaux to this area also.

On our first afternoon, we set the outside table with all the delicious foods that we loved to eat when we had come before on holiday and were looking forward to enjoying again. Two freshly baked baguettes, French salted butter, a selection of French cheeses, a range of cured and cooked ham, olives, tomatoes and, of course, a bottle of our favourite local wine. Lest not forget the *tarte aux poires* that we picked up from one of the local *boulangeries*. Delicious!

The sun was shining; it was 22 degrees. It was December. We were eating outside in the sunshine. We had done it!

We were exhausted. We had a rental car, a rental house, Marc had no job and Beth had still to start school. Minus the weather, we had enjoyed a good lifestyle in Scotland. We always lived in beautiful locations, had beautiful houses that we would have designed by an interior designer to ensure top resale value, we had our choice of cars and money to take us to most locations that we wished to visit. Our daughter was privately educated. You could say that we had 'made it', but we found ourselves living indoors much of the time due to inclement weather. We spent many of our weekends sitting in a café in a children's indoor play area or in a café in a garden centre. It was, to be fair, compared to much of what happens in this world, not a true complaint. Marc and I were truly thankful for everything that we had achieved, but we continued to dream of living somewhere else, preferably in a hot climate.

Marc and I were on an adventure when we first met and although we wished to continue travelling and having fun, with setting up new businesses, life just began to get too serious. We got caught up trying to create the perfect lifestyle; the perfect house in the perfect area, the perfect car, the best school. Our lifestyle choices were not making us happy. Beth was getting caught up in the same competitive chatter that surrounded Marc and I, and it was taking its toll on our happiness as a family unit. We longed to simplify our lifestyle.

As I sat back on our first evening in an old armchair that had been squashed into the small living space, nursing my umpteenth glass of Provençal wine, I looked over at Marc, who had dozed off long ago as he sat snuggled up by Beth on the sofa where they were supposed to be watching a movie together. He was exhausted and I noticed too that he had lost a considerable amount of weight.

Marc grew up enjoying long hot summers in New Zealand, surfing in the Pacific Ocean, and was longing to experience living in the sunshine again. He had spent sixteen years of his life living in Scotland and whilst he was happy enough working there and had made many friends, the lack of sunshine had taken its toll, and when he looks in the mirror and sees his receding hairline, he will always blame it on the lack of sunshine and feels sure that if he had moved to a warmer climate sooner, he would have an abundance of hair. Who am I to argue with that…I don't know… maybe?

Amongst Marc's greatest qualities is that he is an optimist; and when faced with anything negative in his life he will always give careful consideration as to how to turn it around into a positive. I love that about him as it is also the way in which my mind works, thus giving us double the chance of reaching a positive outcome faster.

I looked over to where Beth was with her head against Marc's shoulder as she struggled to keep her eyes open to finish her movie. In front of her on the rug sat her favourite cuddly toys: Pewcat (a black and white cat she fell in love with on her last trip to New Zealand), Yellow Duck (she fell in love with when we were dropping off clothing to a charity shop), and the usual suspects, Minnie, Mickey and Donald, who were all positioned in front of the TV. Her favourite squad.

Beth was nine years of age, a little girl who loved reading Enid Blyton and watching *The Simpsons*. Her favourite meal was breakfast. She loved chocolate, seldom ate sweets, and despised fizzy drinks. She had been an anxious child, and change was not her favourite word, but little by little she was learning to accept that change was necessary if she was ever to experience all the wonders that life has to offer. When we spoke about moving to France, Beth was always included in our conversations, and when we spoke of where we were planning to rent a house, we chose a location that she was familiar with. The previous year we had visited what was to be her new school, an international school in the outskirts of Aix-en-Provence, which would give her the opportunity to continue to speak English as she learnt French on a gradual basis. When we spoke to her about starting school, her face would light up as she knew exactly where she was going and had already met her new head teacher and was now keen to get started. With some careful planning and good communication skills, we were able to ease her anxiety and continue to move on as a family.

It was my dream when I was Beth's age to move country and to have my own swimming pool. As a child, I could seldom think of anything I wanted more.

Two

The decision to move country – aged six

I was six years of age when I made the decision that I was going to move country. I recall the day well. I was upstairs in my bedroom looking down onto our back garden. I remember it being a very hot summer's day. My father was lying back in a small two-ringed blow-up paddling pool with his bathing trunks on, and my brother was jumping in and out splashing our father as my mother sat on a deck chair sunbathing. Believe it or not, this was a scene from Scotland, a rare scene these days but that summer it was particularly hot.

I had been daydreaming, looking out of my window for some time. I was imagining that we had a swimming pool at the back of our garden. It was an inground rectangular pool and the water was blue as it reflected the beautiful blue sky above. In my head, I could clearly see each of my best friends in the pool with me, all jumping about having the best summer ever. When I stopped daydreaming and looked down onto our garden, it was really rather boring, with a small terrace as you exited the back door and climbed up a few stone steps onto a grassed area. To the right was a small pathway with a soil bed to each side where each summer we would grow strawberries. This pathway led to the typical creosoted garden shed. To the rear of the shed there was a section of grass that spanned over to the fence that divided us from our neighbours. It was this area that I felt was perfectly suited for a swimming pool. As I spread my hands up against the glass of my bedroom window to measure out the pool, I felt a surge of excitement. This was the perfect location for a swimming pool. I was one hundred per cent certain everyone was going to love this idea. Why wouldn't they?

I recollect running down the stairs impatiently and out into the back garden, where everyone was still in position. I was bursting with excitement. My father was one of those men who could build or mend anything and I felt sure that installing a pool would be an easy enough task. I reasoned it was only a matter of measuring out the ground and digging a large hole. It seemed like something that was easily created. Maybe even get it completed on a weekend?

"Can we get a real swimming pool?" I asked. "We have lots of room at the top of the garden and it would be amazing." I was beside myself with excitement.

My mother was still half dozing in the heat and I could see her reluctantly opening her eyes and looking at me as if to say, is she still going on about this damned pool?

"Come in the paddling pool, Abi, if you are too hot," shouted my father.

"The paddling pool is too small. We have the room to build a proper one, I have measured it out and there is plenty of space at the top of the garden." I was starting to realise as I spoke to my father that maybe the space at the back of the garden looked bigger from upstairs than it was in reality.

"Abi, it sounds great, but it is not normal for us to experience such a hot summer and it is just too expensive to put in a proper pool," said my mother, who had finally woken up and looked to have thought up a suitable explanation. "It is not the right country for a pool as it isn't always hot enough in Scotland, plus it is just too expensive."

As a six-year-old, the thought process goes along the lines of…we just needed to dig a big hole, line it with concrete, paint it blue and fill it with water. It was the easiest thing in the world. I had witnessed my father building a fence around the front garden, building a wall at the back garden, and creating a small patio/terrace. I had seen him lift out and replace the entire engine of our family Mini, which for a child was an incredible feat; there was nothing this man could not do (in my mind). Obviously, at a young age you have full faith in your father's abilities; therefore, digging a hole couldn't possibly be that hard and how was this going to cost a lot of money?

I accepted what I was told because, let's be honest, back in the day you didn't have too much within you to question your parents, so the best option was to accept the response and get on with your life. However, that did not stop me from considering the negative response and seeing if I could find a positive solution to get the result I so desired.

As a child that grew up in the 1970s, there was always a home catalogue in our house. I was always looking through the catalogue when I was bored, making up my wish list. Normally, I concentrated on the toy section but this day I was extra bored and had started to browse the sports section when I came across two pages selling swimming pools. These ranged from the typical blow-ups to a large collapsible pool that showed the whole family enjoying the space. Mum and Dad in the pool leaning against the side, smiling, one child climbing the ladder, another one having just dived in and another running around wet, chasing the family dog. The pre-Instagram perfect family picture. I looked at the price; I wasn't so sure if it was expensive or not, but I did understand the concept of paying up items from the catalogue as I had heard my mother talking about it. Excitedly, I broke the news to my parents.

"Abi," my mother said gently, "we know that you really want this pool, but we do not live in a hot country so it would get very little use, and we cannot spend that amount of money on something that we would rarely use. Maybe we could just get a slightly bigger blow-up pool."

The one big problem with being a child is that you get no say as to what country you get to live in. I was six years of age and was already unhappy with where I was living. I could not envisage how this was ever going to change.

Fortunately for me one day when I was visiting my grandmother, she had a visitor. The visitor was her niece who a few years previously had moved from my grandmother's village in Scotland to New Zealand. I remember being very shy and chose to look at her through a door that I had slightly ajar between the hallway and the living room. I had never heard of New Zealand but from what she was saying, it sounded to be a place that was very far away. I looked at her as if she had just landed from Mars. When she left, my grandmother explained that Margaret had wanted a change of country and had taken the opportunity to become what would later be referred to as a *£10 POM*, in the early 1960s. This was a one-way £10 ticket on a boat organised by the UK government to encourage emigration to New Zealand. My grandmother explained that whilst she had gotten out there on a cheap voyage, it had taken her several years to save up enough money to come back to the UK to be able to visit her family. She seemed to be happy living in New Zealand and had mentioned to my grandmother that it was a lot warmer there than it was in Scotland. I asked my grandmother if she thought that people in New Zealand had swimming pools in their gardens and she said yes, it was possible. This was to be a life-changing moment for me as here was someone who had also dreamt of moving to a warmer climate and she had done it and seemed happy with her decision.

As I grew up, there was not one moment where I steered off course. I was going to have my swimming pool and I was going to live in a warmer climate. I travelled and explored but as much as I loved many of the countries that I visited, there was not one that I could have called home. I had never travelled as far as New Zealand, and with a friend having emigrated to Australia, I thought it would be a good opportunity to explore the opposite side of my world. With a working visa for Australia secured in my passport, I was ready for a new adventure, but for one reason or another, I decided at the last minute to take the train up to the north of Scotland and find a holiday job in a hotel. For the life of me, I had no idea why I made this decision, but the reason was soon to become apparent.

Three

The search to find home

Marc and I met when we were both twenty-five. He had flown over from New Zealand and had been working in a pub in London and had spent several months travelling through Europe. Having given most of his savings to travel companies, and bar owners, he needed to settle down for a bit to build up his bank account and he chose to do so in the same holiday town in Scotland that I had chosen. We were in fact working five minutes from each other and met one evening at the local backpackers' hostel. It was a stifling hot summer, allowing us to spend many glorious days at the beach and many glorious nights at the pub. We met in June 1995 and saw each other just about every day. He cancelled his plans to tour Spain with his Kiwi mates and I cancelled my Australian trip, and after just four months of our chance meeting we made the ridiculous decision to get married. A small ceremony with only a couple of friends and my immediate family, which amounted to just my father and two sisters, and we were on our way to New Zealand where we had made the decision to set up home. I was so eager to move to a hot climate that I gave no consideration whatsoever as to how far New Zealand was from my family and friends. I was solely focused on myself and the realisation of my childhood dream.

Marc had taken a fair amount of persuasion to head back home as it had taken him several years to find the courage to leave New Zealand in the first place, and here he was leaving his European adventure prematurely with a new wife in tow who his parents had yet to set eyes upon. His dread was arriving back home to find out that nothing had changed from the time he had left.

When travelling to a foreign country, I would always take the time to read up upon where I was going and if the language was different to set aside time to at least learn some basic vocabulary. Please, thank you, can I have a glass of wine, or a beer, were the first on the list. A token attempt that helped me to fit in when I arrived at my destination. On this occasion, because I was going to an English-speaking country and was married to one of their own, I did not envisage having difficulties fitting in because I did not expect the country to where I was heading to be hugely different to the one that I had just left, other than the obvious and major detail of swapping suffocating clouds for blue-sky days.

When we arrived in New Zealand, Marc found that his worst fears were realised as nothing had changed since he had left, and he felt somewhat deflated as he called his previous employer to ask for his old job back. On my side, I had an overwhelming and unexpected feeling that I had landed on the moon; such was the distance that I had put between myself and my beautiful family and friends. I expected to feel at home when I arrived, but instead I felt estranged from the people around me. When I joined a temping agency that gave me the opportunity to work within a university, a hospital and various other offices, I still hoped I could fit in with some bunch or other, but nope, every conversation, no matter where I worked, was always centred around their favourite topic: how New Zealand was the greatest country in the world and how lucky I was to be there. I did not feel lucky. I felt as though I was being spoken to like I had just reached their shores on a crowded dingy having escaped a war-torn country. Were they trying to convince themselves or me? I wondered.

From my viewpoint, the world was having a party since my arrival, and the world had not the courtesy to offer me an invitation, such was my feeling of isolation. I appreciated the beauty of the country and the kindness shown towards me by my new family, but I desperately needed to feel part of something bigger, far bigger, where residents respected people from other countries rather than just their own. Six months after our arrival, we packed up our belongings and bought our one-way ticket back to Scotland. New Zealand was to be kept for holidays and Scotland was a stopgap until we found home.

Fast-forward to 2006 and we were still to be found in Scotland. Financially, our decision to return had played out well enough and we were now living in a beautiful house in a picturesque Scottish village. We had also welcomed our beautiful Beth into our family.

We had travelled extensively with the hope of finding a warmer country to live in. We both adored the Italian lifestyle, yet despite numerous holidays to mainland Italy and Sicily, as well as Sardinia, we never found anywhere that we felt we could call home. We loved our Italian holidays but each time our holiday came to an end we were happy to return to Scotland. We desired to find a country where we felt at home the minute our feet touched the ground.

France was not on our minds at all at this point. Throughout my life I had known many people who had holidayed in France and had loved the country, often opting to return year upon year. Some of my friends liked to spend a weekend in Paris and whilst they each came back with stories of all the incredible museums, cafés, and restaurants they had visited and long descriptions of food and wine consumed, their accounts often concluded with a story of how rude they had found the French to be. This looked to be a common complaint, and a weekend trip to Paris with my friend to see Bruce Springsteen in concert gave me a chance to experience France for myself.

On this fleeting visit, I was surprised to find the French extremely friendly and kind, but upon reflection I had arrived with the attitude that everyone was going to be rude to me, so anything above rudeness was probably seen as delightful. I knew how to say please and thank you and how to order a beer and a glass of wine but that was about the subtotal of my French. I recall waiting in line to purchase my first *crêpe au chocolat* from a small shop situated near the end of the Champs-Élysées. I was feeling rather nervous and a little out of my comfort zone. In front of me was a line of school children varying, I guessed, between the ages of eight and ten and listening to them chatter as they patiently waited for their turn was enchanting, as was the respectful way in which they addressed the server and the great lengths they went to thank him when each *crêpe* was duly wrapped in a white paper napkin and placed into their hands. "*Merci beaucoup, Monsieur,*" they all uttered one by one until it was my turn, and thanks to these beautiful children, I knew exactly how to order my *crêpe* and how I was to respond when I received it.

Speaking French for the first time in France and I felt a tad overwhelmed and embarrassed as I wondered if they would be able to comprehend my Scottish take on their language. I had after all been taught French by a Scottish teacher who pronounced French very differently to what I was now hearing. I was hesitant to speak, and my casual attire of shorts and a tee-shirt was limiting me as to where I could stop for lunch as I peered into some beautiful restaurants with tables decked in fine white linen. If I am brutally honest, my first visit to France left me feeling a little intimidated, and whilst I adored Paris and planned to return, I had no thoughts on this visit that a life in France was going to be on the cards.

Now, having lived amongst the French for so long and being accustomed to their ways, visits to Paris are far more relaxing and enjoyable, plus I have the luxury of tuning into tourists who arrive with their schoolboy French, as they plant their bottoms onto seats at a restaurant without waiting to be seated or enter a busy restaurant at lunchtime to order one lunch to be shared between two and I have a chuckle to myself. In the same way as tourists may leave Paris bemoaning the rudeness of the French, I do feel that if they had just taken the time to learn French etiquette, they would have had a far more rewarding experience. The French as a rule do not tolerate bad manners and they will have no hesitation in correcting you, which I guess forms part of the stories that make their way around the world.

Back in Scotland and Marc and I would often watch the many programmes that were on TV designed to make us all feel dissatisfied with our lives. Tuning into watch people who had traded the UK for Spain, France or Italy, and there we would be, glass of wine in hand, nibbling from the cheese and crackers on the coffee table as we imagined ourselves living far away in the beautiful Italian or French countryside. As we watched the hopeful renovators work away improving their dream house, we would sit there discussing what we would do in their situation and how we would manage and earn money, which was often the difficult element when the people had opted to move country. A reality check at the end of the show would focus on value for money when purchasing a house, whether it be a project, a house with a few adjustments required or walking into a house that was normally over budget but in perfect condition. In some cases, we would watch shows where the family had spent their entire life savings on a remote tumbledown house set in the middle of the French, Spanish or Italian countryside and by the end of the project, when the novelty of living in a remote location had worn off and they had decided to return to the UK, they were up against trying to find a buyer as well as trying to recoup the money that they had outlaid. The decision to buy a project whilst wearing rose-tinted glasses, or more worryingly drinking from a glass containing rose-tinted wine, was proving to be very costly for some.

Now when I think back to these programmes, I picture a savvy French farmer looking at a way to make money and thinking of the old collapsed stone barn in one of his fields. Is it true that the Brits are buying up our old ruins? he asks himself. He has offered the run-down building to his family but, being young, they have their hearts set on a new build and a shopping expedition to IKEA to furnish it. Why would we want to live in an old house, they may ask their father, when we can live in a modern one?

I can imagine him shrugging and speaking with his wife, who may likely be annoyed that her children do not want to live next door where she could see/preside over/supervise/control both her own children and her grandchildren as they grow up. It could go two ways from there: a massive family dispute or relenting and taking out his old Motorola flip phone, to take a photo of the ruin as he considers hocking it off to the Brits. A few weeks later and with a couple of enquiries, he looks to have concluded a sale. On one side of the Channel, with rose-tinted glasses still perched on the end of their noses, a British family who feel that with the reduced offer they got themselves a bargain (dumb French). On the opposite side of the Channel, a savvy French farmer counting his money (dumb Brits).

Fast-forward several months when the new owners take possession of their soon-to-be dream home and have the plans in their hands to go up a level and extend the house to all sides, along with the installation of a pool. All they need now is to get their drawings approved by the local *mairie*. Unbeknown to them, it is likely that the farmer is either friends with the *mairie*, the *mairie* is some distant cousin, or the farmer is the *mairie*. Should the plans be accepted and should the family be able to find good-quality tradesmen who turn up when asked and do not rip them off, they are doing well, especially if they can put up with the farmer's family standing in their garden first thing in the morning as they wait to tell them what they can and cannot do with the house (guaranteed). Whilst the sale has concluded, to the farmer and his family the house and the land remain theirs.

Returning to May 2006, Beth was soon to turn four and we knew that if we were going to relocate, we had better get a move on, but we were all out of ideas until one day I received a surprise phone call from Marc, who was working at a client's house.

"Abi, Linda's husband works with a guy in Dubai who has a house in the South of France, somewhere near Cannes. He is looking for someone to renovate it. What do you think, should I get in touch with him?" he asked.

I was taken aback but it sounded like a great adventure. "Of course," I replied. "Get in touch and see if this is just talk or something that he really wants to run with." It was sounding too good to be true.

Several weeks later and Marc was on his way to France. I sat patiently by the phone, desperate to receive a call to hear how he was getting on. The phone finally rang.

"Abi, you would not believe where I am. I am eating in a restaurant in Cannes." Marc was truly excited, which was somewhat out of character. "It is beautiful here," he exclaimed, "and I have agreed to take on the job. We are just discussing about a second visit so that you can come out to help me measure up. Are you up for it?"

Of course I was up for it. I could not book our flights quick enough.

Several weeks later, Marc, Beth and I arrived at Nice Airport. It was early springtime and our aeroplane had huffed and puffed to fight its way through the thick layers of cloud that hung low over Edinburgh Airport. To our amazement, as we approached Nice there was not a cloud in sight. With a perfect landing in perfect conditions, as we walked down the stairs of the aeroplane, we felt we had travelled much further than the two and a half hours' flying time. It was another world. I can honestly say that I fell in love with the South of France the moment I arrived.

We had a few busy days ahead of us as we spent our time measuring up our client's house and detailing the building materials that would be required. As Marc and I both felt the same way now towards the South of France, we decided to take some time off to go sightseeing. The first place that we visited was Antibes. My youngest sister had won a French-speaking competition when she was eighteen and was based in Nice for a week, where she used the opportunity to explore Antibes. She told us that we could not go to the South of France without a visit to this beautiful area. She explained that it was an ancient coastal town famous for its Roman and Greek architecture and that we simply had to visit the castle and cathedral. The sun was high in the sky, not a cloud to be seen. The beach had a scattering of people. It was around 20 degrees in the sunshine and there were some children paddling in the sea. Early spring in the South of France I could see was high summer in Scotland.

I had spent several weeks prior to coming over to France this time expanding my vocabulary, and felt confident enough to leave Marc and Beth on the beach whilst I went on the search for a *boulangerie* to buy lunch. On the way to the *boulangerie*, a friendly waiter shouted over to me as he stood by the entrance of his restaurant. As he spoke to me, I realised that whilst I may have broadened by French vocabulary, my ability to understand spoken French had not improved and I had not made out one single word. My newfound confidence was gone in a flash as I stood there staring at him, trying desperately to remember the saying that I am now rather famous for: "*Pardon, Monsieur. Je parle petit peu Francais.*" With that, he laughed and quickly started to speak to me in English, which seemed the easiest thing in the world to him. It was to be my first taste of the flirtatious antics of a French waiter as they bid to bring in their clientele.

There were many *boulangeries* surrounding the beach area to choose from, each very busy. The display of food put most bakeries that I had visited in my lifetime to shame. Squares of pizzas, *croque monsieurs*, filled baguettes, plus of course the usual *patisseries*, a wide selection of freshly baked bread and baguettes, and my eyes just about jumped out of their sockets when I spotted the finest selection of cakes that I had ever seen in my life. I could see that the French took the creation and display of their food very seriously.

Selecting from the display presented to me was not an easy task. I had to choose what I wanted, which meant I had also to speak, and there was a queue now in front of me and behind me and everyone seemed to be talking very quickly. My turn was quickly coming around.

« *Celui-ci, sil vous plaît* » I quickly uttered as I pointed one at a time to what I wished to purchase. Much to my delight, she looked to have understood my utterings and with renewed confidence I selected a filled baguette, a *croque monsieur*, a slice of pizza and a selection of cakes that I thought would delight Marc and Beth. What a relief, but I also wanted to order coffee. "*Je voudrais café, s'il vous plaît,*" I said nervously, hoping that I had got this right, and sure enough I was directed to the opposite end of the shop where someone was waiting to take my drinks order.

"*Une café avec lait et une café noir, s'il vous plaît.*" (A coffee with milk and a black coffee, please.) The lady gave me an odd look and responded with words that could equally have been in Chinese. I had made an error. I was in a predicament, and I needed quickly to get out of it, so sensing that she was asking me a question, I responded with "*Oui*" and nodded my head to confirm my answer. Soon enough, I was given two coffees and hoped that one had milk and the other black, but at this stage anything would have been fine as I scurried out of the shop juggling my purchases.

On my walk back to the beach, I had a large grin on my face. My French wasn't great, I admitted to myself, but I still got what I set out to buy and I was inwardly proud of my achievement. My self-congratulating was interrupted by a car that had pulled up to my side, and with windows rolled down, a French tourist had stopped to ask me for something which I presumed to be directions. "*Pardon, Monsieur. Je parle petit peu Francais.*" He smiled and said something in response which I could not make out, and as he pulled away, my grin expanded. Bloody glad I learnt that line, I thought to myself. Not only had I spoken French today, but I also looked like a local. I was in a foreign country and yet for once I was fitting in. What joy!

Our lunch was truly scrumptious and afterwards Beth got the chance to splash about happily in the water with the other children whose parents had taken them to the beach for a picnic lunch. Coffee, thankfully, was exactly as I had wanted, which was more luck than anything else. Gone were any thoughts of exploring the local attractions. We had far more important things to discuss, such as how were we going to make France our home?

When we arrived back in Scotland, there was a lot of work to do selecting and organising all the building materials which we were sending out on a removal lorry to Cannes. Marc arranged to fly out to meet the driver and had some tradesmen that he knew come out too. As the work commenced, Marc would phone me each night as he sat having some beers by the pool after working in the hot sun each day. He was having the time of his life.

Our client's house was a ten-minute drive from Cannes. It was a simple single-storey house with three good-sized bedrooms, one with ensuite, a living and dining room area with kitchen and a main bathroom. A small lawned garden to the front and climbing up a small hill to the back of the house, hidden behind some trees, lay a medium-sized oval inground swimming pool. It was a simple yet charming French house with its own gated driveway, with the house being tucked behind a large wall that covered the circumference of their land, giving the house a feeling of secrecy, being hidden away quietly from the surrounding shops. A visit to the local estate agent helped us to see that this was affordable for us if we were able to find a similar income to what we were earning in Scotland. There was hope!

The construction of houses down in the south is either of traditional stone that has stood the test of time for many hundreds of years or modern block. As a traditional self-employed joiner, Marc included the building of extensions in Scotland, but these were all built with a timber frame before being bricked. It was not the same in France and therefore finding work would prove challenging. Marc also had been working for himself for many years; the thought of starting again was mind-boggling, especially when you built into this the need to learn another language.

We had a lot to consider. We had no plans to jump at this early stage. Our previous experience told us to take it slow and to explore France at our own pace to see if we continued to feel at home and if we could find a way to earn a living.

Beth was our priority and we had promised her that we would find her an English-speaking school initially to allow her to learn French, so that would narrow down where we could live. At this point also, amid selling our home and moving to another renovation project in Scotland, there was the housing crash of 2008. It was predicted to happen in Scotland and whilst Marc and I had discussed it on many occasions, we chose to power on through and to remain positive. On this occasion, remaining positive was to be our financial downfall.

The short version of this ghastly time was that we simply cut our losses and sold our house for a fraction more than we paid for it, considering that we had added an extension and had it completely renovated. We had signed on a house which had now dropped substantially in value, but we were legally tied in and had to agree a settlement to allow us to pull out of the sale. The result was that instead of moving into our final renovation project to catapult us to France, we were left with debt and living in a rented cottage.

Marc and I are hugely motivated people and are never down for long. We reflected that the same desire and positivity that lost us our money was also what made us our money, and that with lessons learnt we would find another way to find the money to take us to France. From the housing crash of 2008, it took us another five years to get our affairs in order and to have sufficient funds to make a move viable. By this time, we had come over to the South of France on four separate occasions for family holidays and Marc on a further two occasions to complete additional work for his client.

One day in the summer of 2013, as we sat outside in the sunshine having a BBQ lunch, we made the unanimous decision that we were to move to France by the end of the year. Time was ticking away, and Beth was getting to the stage where she thought we were never going to move and was getting frustrated with our endless chatter. She had just turned nine and we could not leave it any longer if she was to adapt to French life. She had been attending private French lessons and was picking it up well, and with a transition to an international school that we had already visited on our last holiday, we all felt that the time was as right as it was ever going to be.

Our money situation wasn't great. We had saved up £20,000. We had two rental houses that, once overheads were paid, brought us in an additional £600 per month. We had paid off our debt but nonetheless opting to move to another country with such little funds was taking a huge gamble. We reasoned that when we met, we each had very little in our bank accounts, and within a few years of hard work we had turned that around quickly. If we could do it before, we could, without doubt, do it again. We were more determined than ever.

December 2013. Everything was going to plan. We had decided to hire a Luton box van from London to take our essential items that would allow us to furnish a small house and to leave the rest of our worldly possessions with a removal and storage company in Scotland. Our thought process was for Marc to fly down to London to collect the van and for us all to drive over to France together.

Our last night, everything was packed up in the van and we were sitting on boxes enjoying a Chinese takeout and a glass or two of Côtes du Rhône.

"Have you by any chance seen Beth's passport, Abi?" asked Marc.

"Have you checked your bedside cabinet?" I replied, rather shocked at the question that had been presented to me.

"Yes, I have checked but it wasn't there. I thought maybe you had taken it out and put it somewhere." Marc replied.

"I wish I had, but no, I haven't seen it, and if it is not in your drawer then I have no idea as to where it could be," I replied. With the impending move, our nerves were already fraying and I could feel my stress levels rising as I contemplated the oncoming drama.

By this stage, just about everything was packed up and stacked inside the van. It was not easy to reach the bedside cabinet drawers that were surrounded now with heavy boxes and as we finally lifted enough items out of the van to reach the cabinets, our temporary relief at having got to them was taken over with the horror of the passport not being within them. What on earth were we going to do? Marc was always the one who gathered the passports together for each of our holidays and each of our passports were always stored in the top drawer of his bedside cabinet. We never stored them anywhere else.

"Beth," I asked, "remember we kept your passport in Dad's drawer beside his bed? Do you remember going in and taking your passport out?"

"Yes, sometimes I went up to the drawer and looked at my passport, but I always put it back in." Beth replied.

Children can be so easily distracted, and I realised that Beth could easily have looked at her passport and placed it on the bed instead of back inside the drawer. If that was the case, it was likely that her passport had been packed away into one of the boxes that we had placed on the bed when we were packing up. The problem was that half of the boxes were in the van and the other half in storage.

The storage facility that we had selected was in Dumfries, a two and a half hours' drive from our house, but it was within a removal company and not a self-storage unit, so we would have to wait until it was open during office hours to ask them to search through our boxes. We put our bottle of Côtes du Rhône to one side as we sat contemplating our unexpected situation. Beth was very excited about travelling in the van down to Dover and was looking forward to waking up in the morning to enjoy a cooked breakfast. Beth loved having breakfast in a hotel, so much so that we would often take her to a local hotel for a buffet breakfast as a treat. Whatever the new plan was, we had to include a cooked breakfast. There was also the much-anticipated ferry ride and the second hotel stop-off, which offered a continental breakfast, which she was also looking forward to. A change in travel arrangements was not going to be easy.

We knew realistically that the chances of finding the passport were slim and that the best course of action was to apply for a fast-track passport, which would mean taking a trip into Glasgow. We were trying desperately to conserve money and as we had hired a van and booked all the hotels and ferry crossings, it made better financial sense for Marc to continue with the travel plans, but it was clear at this stage that these plans were not going to include Beth and I. Marc was eager to get going and quickly phoned around some friends to see who was available for a last-minute trip to France. Finally, with a little bit of luck on our side, Marc received a yes from his friend Chris. Whilst we went to bed with heavy hearts, we woke up more determined than ever to get our plans back on track. We packed up the last of our things, a final clean-up, and we headed over to my father's for lunch.

I had pre-warned my father and his wife that they were to expect two frazzled adults and one bewildered child. We did not disappoint.

The ferry was booked for late the following morning, so Marc did have some time up his sleeve and after a short sleep he left at 4am to collect Chris and to get on with their long journey ahead.

This left Beth and I to try and sort out her new passport. With passport photos in hand, we took the train into Glasgow the following morning and headed for the passport office. Our clerk was very helpful and patient, especially when he had to endure listening to all my woes. I had my hopes up that we could secure a new passport that day or even the next, but when he broke the news that it may take up to a week, it was all too much for Beth.

"No, I want to go to France today. Please can I have my new passport today?" Tears were streaming down her face. My poor girl was exhausted.

I quickly whispered in her ear, "Would you like to go for a cooked breakfast?" and with that a little smile appeared.

"Café Rouge?"

"Of course!" I replied.

Over our breakfast we debated how we could turn our newfound situation into a memorable adventure. My sister had been raving to me about the wonders of the Christmas market in Edinburgh and so I suggested this to Beth.

"What if we were to take the train to Edinburgh and book a beautiful hotel, visit the Christmas market and explore all the toy shops, what do you think?" I asked.

"Oh, Mum, that sounds amazing. Yes, let's do it." A twinkle had appeared in her eyes again.

We certainly had a memorable adventure in Edinburgh. Although it was cold, the sun was shining. The Christmas market was indeed beautiful and worth visiting, as were the toy shops. Cooked breakfast each morning and pizza in the evenings, and as we lay on our shared bed we would each take turns to make up ghost stories, which would make us both laugh; nervous laughter from two tired and exhausted individuals, but laughter was better than the alternative.

Marc and Chris had phoned to say that they had arrived safely at our rental property in France. They had dropped off our personal items, and the rest of our furniture and personal effects they spent an afternoon loading into a storage unit in Aix-en-Provence. Finally, on the verge of collapse, they had telephoned us to say that they were enjoying a few beers on the terrace sitting in the warm winter sunshine.

Back in Edinburgh, I remember sitting in the restaurant area in John Lewis enjoying our festive lunch when we received the phone call from my father that Beth's passport had finally arrived and that he was on his way to the airport to deliver it to us. My sister had gone ahead to book our flights to travel to

London. Much needed family support that created order in a time of chaos.

Sometimes, though, when things start off wrong, they just keep going down the same track. Our flight from Edinburgh to London was postponed by five hours! I looked at my exhausted little girl and felt a pang of guilt. What were we doing? Why were we putting her through this? Were we crazy parents? If you were a person who looked for signs, all the signs were there to cancel our trip, but in our hearts we still knew that despite what had happened, we were making the right decision. We reasoned to ourselves that it was a test.

Our flight finally took off in the small hours of the morning. We arrived at our airport hotel in London around 2:30am where Marc was waiting at the front door to greet us. Marc had driven back to London the previous day; Chris had flown back to Scotland, and we were finally back together as a family. What a joyous moment.

A quick shut-eye and up at 5am to catch the 7am flight to Marseille.

Our plane cruised through the clear blue sky and onto the runway. When we disembarked and walked down onto the tarmac, it was with joy that we felt the heat of the morning sun on our tired and worn faces. We strolled over to the car park in the glorious sunshine to retrieve our hire car and an hour later we pulled up at what was to be our new home for the next three and a half months. Despite everything that we felt was thrown at us, there we were eating what was to be the first of many delicious lunches under the rays of the glorious Provençal sunshine.

Four

Adapting to French life

Christmas Eve, 2013. It is 22 degrees, and we are lounging on a beach in Marseille munching our way through various delights we have purchased from a well-stocked *boulangerie* across from the beach. We had to nip ourselves to remind us that we had made it to France and that, no, this was not a dream. As we each sat there quietly in our own little world, we could hear people behind us laughing and as we turned around to follow where the noise was coming from, we saw a group of teenagers strip off to their undies and run past us, one by one, as they dived straight into the sea. I doubted the water would be anything close to warm but as I have adapted to French life, I have found that the French find any excuse to head to the beach to have a dip in the Med and I have learnt to follow suit.

We had made the decision to consider the stretch of time between the day of our arrival and the day Beth started school as a family holiday. We had hired a small rental car and were spending our days exploring all our old haunts. Many of these included favourite restaurants and *boulangeries* as well as beaches that we longed to revisit. On holiday, there can often be that pang of despair when you realise that the time is fast approaching when you must board the aircraft or pack up the car and return home. The gloom that can darken the last couple of days of a holiday can be due to leaving hot sunshine for rain or the thought of returning to work. On this occasion, whilst we had no pressure to return to the UK and were desperately convincing ourselves that everything would work out in the end, there was certainly no escaping the fact that we were all stressed and pretty much wired to the moon.

The house we were living in was designed by our neighbour/ landlord, who had chosen to include the construction of a secondary property attached to their own to allow for a little extra cash during the summer months. Jean and Rose were a retired couple who had planned their retirement meticulously. They had the rental property we were living in plus a well-equipped modern campervan that was parked to the front of their house which they used for their casual commute to their apartment in Portugal. As we got to know them better, they informed us that their son continued to live in their apartment in Bordeaux. The use of the word *apartment* was used in a humble style on this occasion as flicking through their photo album this simple description translated in reality to a quarter of a château set in the midst of an exquisite landscaped garden with swimming pool. This was where they spent Christmas and New Year.

Jean and Rose were down-to-earth, kind, welcoming and utterly charming. They simply could not do enough to help us as we adjusted to our new life. We were taken aback by their hospitality and appreciated their invitation to share a meal with them only two days after our arrival. In truth, both Beth and I wished only to spend the week fast asleep tucked up in our own beds as we were worn out, but we accepted their invitation nonetheless as it would have been rude not to. Thankfully, it was a casual meal with crudités, saucisson and sliced baguette placed in the centre of the table as our entrée, followed by sliced pork in a cream sauce with mashed potatoes and a selection of vegetables. At the end of our main course, I looked over to see Beth just about sliding off her seat and if I had left her any longer I am sure she would have slid right off and fallen asleep under the table, so I made my motherly excuses to take her home whilst Marc stayed on to enjoy dessert. There would have to be an alien invasion or a threat of a nuclear war for Marc to skip dessert.

Our first Christmas in France and I cannot remember for the life of me what we ate that year. I cannot recall roasting a turkey but that is not to say that I did not do so. Our thoughts were always elsewhere as our brains worked overtime thinking through our situation and coming up with ideas and possible solutions. We were unable to knock off without the help of a few glasses of wine to aid sleep and in the morning, we used coffee to switch our brains back on. Not the healthiest option and I knew this would take its toll.

I had my own small business that I adapted to allow me to work from home, and that at least was contributing to Beth's school fees, plus the money from our two UK rentals that covered our rent in France. Our £20,000 wasn't likely to stretch that far with still having to buy a van and a car, so we had to find a way for Marc to earn money quickly.

It was Thursday, 2 January, and our self-proclaimed holiday had concluded, as it was to be Beth's first day at her new school. We had chosen an International School and as I mentioned previously, we had already taken Beth to visit her new school on our last holiday, so she knew exactly where she was going. I remember the difficulty that we had locating the school on our first visit. Surely a school could not be located so far into the countryside but sure enough, down some very narrow, windy roads we went and finally up a rough track we saw on the right what appeared to be a car park. We parked and walked up a rough-looking track and there at the end of the track lay the school. It was a large typically French stone three-storey farmhouse, with crackled pale blue shutters on each window. There was bunting pinned high on the front terrace blowing about in the wind. To the side of the school there were wooden picnic tables for the children to eat their lunch when the weather was good and at the opposite side of the schoolhouse there was a large closed-in lean-to that housed long farmhouse tables and chairs for when the weather was inclement. Our brief tour of the school had taken us down past the main converted farmhouse and down into a rectangular area where they had built several wooden schoolrooms plus an additional small wooden hut that contained the library. The space in the middle of the classroom area formed part of the playground, which ran up past the classrooms up onto the hill and into the woodland, providing plenty of room for adventures.

Finding the school this time around was easy enough. As we walked down to the school, there were lots of children running around, play fighting and just having a heap of fun. I had thought maybe that Beth would want Marc and I to stay close by, but she appeared comfortable with her new surroundings and surprisingly she sent us packing.

Marc and I headed off to a *boulangerie* for breakfast; it is not always easy to combine a coffee with a pastry as not every village has a café. It is acceptable however in many of the establishments that open early for morning coffee for workers to bring in pastries that have been purchased at the local *boulangerie*. The French look to be lax about that kind of thing, but I would certainly ask if it would be okay to do so first as sometimes they will buy the pastries for you and charge a little extra. As we ate our breakfast, the conversation concentrated on Beth as we were both concerned about whether she would be able to cope with all the recent changes in her life.

Finally, after what seemed like the longest day in the world to us both, we returned to collect her. As we waited with all the other parents on the front terrace, we could see the teacher approaching to open the classroom door and, as expected, out bolted Beth. She hesitated for a moment as she searched through all the unfamiliar faces until she spotted us, and when she did she ran up and threw her arms around us as tears started to pour down her face.

Thankfully, her teacher came forward to us to explain that Beth had experienced a difficult day, crying and distressed, but little by little she was able to settle down and things were not so bad come the end of the day. On the way home, Beth offered her own explanation. She was happy when she was dropped off, she assured us both, and all was good until lunchtime when she had taken out her lunch box containing her usual ham sandwiches only to be told by some authoritarian figure that packed lunches were not to be brought to school. It was explained to her that the chef had prepared a lunch that everyone was to partake of, and unless she had an allergy there were to be no exceptions. Being a fussy eater, Beth was instantly ill at ease and it was at this point that she started to cry and wished she had never left the UK. She had been eating ham sandwiches for lunch for the past four years with no interference from anyone until this point. She explained that she had eaten the small pieces of baguette that were served with the meal and putting a napkin over the food she had reluctantly accepted on her plate, she had quietly emptied the contents into the bin. She was, however, rather proud (a grin did appear for a moment) that she had gotten away with it, as the children had been told that there was to be no food waste and she had broken a rule.

"What was the food on the menu, Beth?" we asked as she complained about how hungry she was and how she was unable to concentrate in class in the afternoon due to her grumbling stomach and the thought of having to go through the same the following day and the day after that, and the more she thought about it, the more she cried. It was going to be a long ass journey back home!

"I don't know, but it was a hot lunch, and I was too scared to try it," she replied in between the sobs. "I just want to eat my ham sandwiches."

"You must still have your ham sandwiches in your bag. You can eat them on the way home," I replied as I looked into the mirror. I could see that the thought had already occurred to her and there she was with her bag on her lap, lunch box open, hungrily stuffing a ham sandwich into her mouth.

Once Beth knew what was expected of her, she reasoned to herself that she would need to eat if she was hungry and decided to give certain foods a try if she deemed them to be edible. Slowly and surely, as the days turned into weeks, she would speak to us about all the different foods that she was trying and to my astonishment she would ask me to recreate these meals at home, and so it was that Beth stopped being a fussy eater. There were to be reasonable exceptions, such as the day to her absolute horror they put a boiled egg with spinach on her plate, or a Friday when they insisted upon serving fish. So as not to repeat our first journey home, I opted to keep a bag of snacks in the car just in case.

All her lessons were conducted in English, and French was taught as a foreign language. In the classroom Beth explained that the children were allowed to express themselves freely and were seldom in trouble or even corrected. One day as I ran up to gather Beth into my arms at the end of the school day, she was full to the brim of chat and excitedly talked to me about running about in the forest at breaktime, which joined onto a story about a classmate who had been playing up and was told by the teacher to put a sock in it. To Beth's delight, her classmate removed his shoe, then his sock, and proceeded to stuff his sock into his mouth.

The class were in uproar and to Beth's surprise the teacher also found it to be funny. Beth was at first reluctant to laugh as she thought she may get into trouble, but she sensed a different type of class atmosphere than she had been used to. Her teacher was quick to explain that at her school, children were encouraged to be themselves and not to be sheep as it was perfectly acceptable for them to all have their own ideas and opinions. Up until now, Beth had always been in a school environment that encouraged all the children to dress and behave in the same manner. In this school, as is common in France, there were no school uniforms and there were no children coming to school in 'designer-labelled clothes'. Children were allowed to be children. It was a healthy environment for our free-spirited child.

With Beth settled, Marc and I could concentrate our efforts on getting to know some of the parents. There were many opportunities to strike up a conversation as we parked our cars and walked up the rough track to stand and wait on the terrace under the hot sun. As we got talking, we learnt that many of the British parents had in fact come to Provence only for the year. Peter Mayle's book *A Year in Provence* was mentioned on several occasions, and whilst I had not read the book, I did think that it must have contained something exceptional to have given many of the people around us the idea to come over to sample French life. It is only upon reflection that I wonder if Peter's title may have held a subliminal message.

Other parents explained they had relocated for unspecified periods of time based upon work contracts. A large company located within an hour of the school looked to be offering employment to many of the parents. We met families from the UK, Australia, Sweden, Israel, India and America. There was clear excitement on the faces of the parents, who spoke about their amazing time living in Provence and how they had enjoyed day after day of glorious hot weather, and with many opting to have rented houses with outdoor swimming pools, there was the added joy of lazing by the pool and, of course, sampling local wines with their evening BBQs. We spoke to some parents who were near the end of their year in Provence and were openly reluctant to return to their old lives, but despite enjoying an outdoor swimming pool and spending long hot summers running around outside, their children, when asked, simply wished to return home to be with their friends.

With so many children coming and going in that school, I did feel for the teachers. Some of the students could speak neither English nor French and found themselves in a very awkward situation trying to learn both languages simultaneously. We were thankful that Beth had at least a basic understanding of French and appeared to be adapting well to her new way of life.

It was around the fourth week of school and Beth had been invited to a birthday party hosted by an Israeli family. I wondered if she would accept their invitation, because she barely knew the girl who had invited her, and we had yet to meet her parents. To our surprise, she had agreed to go along and was rather excited about attending. The parents asked for the children to be dropped off as they had planned an afternoon full of activities and for the parents to return later in the afternoon for drinks and snacks. That seemed like a sound plan. I made sure to give them my telephone number and headed back home. When I returned, the garden was full of mums and dads chatting away with a glass of wine or beer in their hands. A bonfire looked to be starting in the corner, placed upon what looked like an upturned metal bath. I couldn't figure out what was going on until one by one the children started to exit through the kitchen door with something flat on a paper plate. Responding to my enquiries, one of the parents explained that the children had been making pitta dough and it was now time to cook it, hence the upturned bath. As I cradled my glass of wine, I watched as the father of the birthday girl, took the portion of flattened dough from each child and one by one threw them onto the bathtub. In a flash, they were ready and placed on the waiting table which had been set up with paper plates and several jars of Nutella. Once the children had eaten up their desserts, it was time for the adults to have a go, as the mother had made extra dough for everyone. I have to say that it was the finest pitta bread I have ever tasted, especially with the addition of Nutella. Still to this day, Beth and I salivate when we recount that afternoon.

As we slowly got to know the other parents, Marc and I were often asked why we had made the decision to move to France on a permanent basis since unlike many of them we had no work contracts or businesses continuing to run back in our home country to fund our adventure (albeit we did have our two small rental houses). We always replied in the same vein; we wanted to live a simpler life and to get away from the competitive way of life that we had previously bought into. Sometimes, I could sense that some of the parents were missing their competitive lifestyles and would drop into the conversation the size of property they had waiting back home, or as one mother casually put it as she giggled, "You have got to show off a bit to those back home."

Marc and I had found the competitive chatter back in the UK demoralising. Questions such as, where do you live? What street do you live on? What do you do for a living? What does your husband do? What school does your child attend? What car do you drive? Where are you going on holiday this year? Seemingly innocent and perfectly normal questions until you observe the face of your interrogator, and as you watch their manner and listen to their responses it becomes abundantly clear that they are attempting to work out if they are above or below you in the social rankings. The good old UK class system at its finest/worst, where everyone believes they are middle class as they clamber to afford their Range Rover so they can, mentally at least, propel themselves into aristocracy and take further pleasure in peering down on the poor waifs from a far greater height. It reminds me of something I read in a book somewhere, when the author said that it is a weakness of humans that once they have a roof over their heads and enough food to eat, they concentrate on finding a way to be better than those around them.

The choice for us to exit the UK and move to France was a chance to slow down our lives, opting to live as we each saw fit, and to live quietly. We had no plans to show off, however, in our unstable financial situation and being frazzled with new health issues arising from this, we doubted that anyone would have been envious of our lives.

With Beth now settled at school, the next priority on our never-ending to-do list was to buy two vehicles. Renting was quickly gobbling up our savings.

Marc had tracked himself down a transit van from a garage he found on the outskirts of Cannes, a garage that sold off ex-pharmaceutical delivery vans. His limited budget did not create a wider range and so that afternoon he was left standing in a car yard in Cannes making his selection between three transit vans, each having done galaxy miles, each with residue of old signage and each with various dents. The one he selected had to be jump started, but once it got going, it seemed fine and so a purchase was made. There was to be no credit as we had no financial record in France, so cash it was.

I would be telling humungous lies if I said that searching for my car had any trace of excitement attached to it for me. I was in banger territory, considering that second-hand cars in France kept their price. I was beyond depressed and had just about given up and was searching out bus stops when I spied in a car yard in the back of beyond a purple-coloured Alfa Romeo 147. It was twelve years old but in excellent condition with low mileage. I was over the moon. The garage was asking 5,000€ which was a touch over what we hoped to spend, and we knew back in the UK a car of this age could be bought for under 1,000 GBP, so Marc talked the manager down and finally we were able to secure our Alfa for 4,000€, which we were delighted with.

It was now early February and with vehicles ticked off our list, the next step was to find a permanent home.

As we started to visit estate agents, we realised that we were being quickly dismissed. Our grasp of the language wasn't great, so we were unsure as to why we were not being entertained. A few Google searches later and it became apparent that for us to rent we had to show tax documents for the last two years, preferably in French. The problem was that Marc had closed his business in the UK, I was continuing to work but my business was still UK based and my income was inadequate. We were wakening up to the reality that we had failed to give this matter sufficient attention before we crossed the Channel. We had secured a holiday rental easily enough, but this was for holidays, not for the long term. We continued to ride the wave of positivity, but positivity didn't always cut it. Sometimes in life you need something out of the blue to bring you to attention.

On our various visits to this part of Provence, we were continually charmed by a little antique shop that tended to have something, as we would call it, 'show-stopping' on the outside terrace that would cause us to pull our car over for a closer inspection. Normally, we would just stop the car, get out, ooh and aah and hop straight back in the car.

This day, we were so taken aback as we drove by that we felt almost obliged to stop and talk to the owner. We were so stricken by this beautiful statue. We pulled over our car, got out and crunched our way up the path towards the entrance. Upon entering the shop, we were warmly received by a man who I guess was around the age of Marc and myself. We didn't expect him to understand English but when he started to speak to us in French and picked up on our startled-rabbit look, he quickly changed from French to English, which took us by surprise. His English wasn't great and he himself came across as a startled rabbit the more we spoke to him, but together in our broken French and broken English we managed to have a conversation… of sorts.

I never gave the visit any further thought, but it was clear that this was not the case with Marc, who announced a week or so later that he intended to call down to the antique shop again to see if the proprietor knew of any rentable houses in the area. He had a strong feeling that the owner may well know of a house that we could rent.

The following Saturday morning, Marc got up early and disappeared. Later that morning, I heard him entering the house and as I opened my eyes there he stood at the bedroom door.

"Well, any luck?" I asked as I continued to lay in bed, ready to expect either type of news. Whether it be good or bad news, with Marc there was always the element of having to drag it out of him as his face never always conveyed which type of news it was. With me, on the other hand, with the faint sniff of good news I have a bottle of fizz ready and waiting to open. I waited patiently for his response.

"The owner of the shop is called Clément, who told me that his father owns a house that we could rent. It is in the next village to the one that he lives in, but the only problem is that the house is currently chock-a-block full of antiques. Clément was quick to take me out to see the house and it looks fine to me, but I don't know if you would like it," explained Marc.

I was excited but I was also in a state of anxiety as taking this house all hinged upon his response to my next question. Just as I was about to speak, Marc added:

"Yes, Abi, it does have a pool, but it hasn't been used in several years and it does not come with the house despite being in the attached garden." He paused for effect and smiled as he continued. "I will certainly ask if we can use it as I don't see why not."

It was like a weight being lifted off my shoulders. I was going to get my pool, I just knew it!

We jumped into our Alfa and drove out to a small village that was twenty-five minutes further from Beth's school. The school run was already taking fifty minutes in the busy morning rush hour, and I had hoped to find a house closer rather than further away. If I was honest, I was slightly deflated, but I was also realistic about our situation and our weakened ability to rent and I knew that I could not afford to be fussy.

We drove down a road that I was familiar with but to my surprise Marc pulled up our car alongside a large traditional stone farmhouse that was perched alongside the main road. It was not the idyllic surroundings I had envisaged but nonetheless, as I glanced over the house, it was beautiful, with pale blue shutters adorning each window, matching perfectly the pretty ornate iron railings that surrounded the house. It was exquisite. When we had ideas of coming to France, it was a house such as this that we had imagined ourselves living in, albeit not positioned next to a main road. I could feel that I was going to have to compromise.

The house that the proprietor was proposing to rent to us was attached to a larger house, and I was confused as to what we were being offered to rent and who would be living next door. As we stepped out of the car, we peered directly into the front terrace of the house that Marc had been shown just a couple of hours previously. It was a small dusty terrace no greater than 15 square metres housing a large tree that looked to have been recently crudely pruned. Clément had explained to Marc that the small terrace was the only garden that came with the house. This was disappointing news as surrounding this little terrace lay the most astounding garden that catapulted me back to the book *The Secret Garden* by Frances Hodgson Burnett. A combination of oak and pine trees carefully planted around the border several decades ago and now reaching high into the blue sky gave the garden that wonderful feeling where you want to run around to explore every nook and cranny. Someone had built a traditional dyke wall that looked to intentionally divide the garden into two areas. The left side closest to the proposed rental house was mostly grassed, which I felt would make a terrific spot to play badminton, and surrounding the grassed area what looked to be a selection of fruit trees. It was only guesswork on my part as to what these could possibly be. I could identify cherry, plum and what was possibly a hazelnut tree, but that was sadly the subtotal of my knowledge. A hot summer and these trees would burst into life, exhibiting their fruit and requiring no guesswork on my part. As I stood in amongst these beautiful trees in this idyllic garden, I imagined myself picking the fruit from the trees, making jam and a host of desserts, and I knew at this point that this garden had my name on it. If it had my name on it, I knew it would be mine.

On the right side of the wall, from where I was standing it was impossible to see what was behind it as it was clear that the wall had been built to give this area complete privacy. From what Marc had told me, I knew this garden housed a pool and now I knew where it was hiding.

A wonderful feeling came over me as I felt that somehow this house, the garden and the pool had been sitting here anticipating our arrival. I smiled over to Marc and nodded.

Just at that moment, an old white Citroen C15 van pulled up outside the house and I recognised Clément instantly as he opened the van door and stepped out, introducing himself. Out of the passenger door stepped a man who was the spitting image of Clément, with an additional twenty years or so added on. Clément introduced us to his father. Clément was around 5ft 7" with short black hair and eyes that had mischief engrained into them and a smile to match. He had a slightly protruding stomach as looks to be common in this age group in France. Ditto his father, with the addition of deeper lines in his face and grey/white hair.

I watched as Clément introduced his father, Jean-Baptiste, and observed how he interacted with him in a very respectful and formal manner. The way in which they spoke with each other reminded me of the Victorian way in which I guess children would speak with their fathers, waiting to be spoken to rather than speaking first. I couldn't help but feel I had stepped back in time. As they spoke together in French, Clément seemed very eager to please his father and as they discussed us renting the house, I was gathering very quickly that the idea of banknotes crossing his father's palm was the element behind the smile that started at one ear and finished at the other.

With all the introductions and weather discussions done and dusted, Clément explained that the part of the farmhouse that we were looking to rent belonged to his father, and the house attached to ours, facing the main road, had been lived in by his parents until recently but with this half being owned by his mother, she had bequeathed the house several months back to his brother Antoine. There was a look of despair on the faces of both Clément and his father at this point, both shaking their heads with the mention of his brother. I wondered what the story could be. Clément went onto explain that it was only his brother that lived next door and that he seldom had any visitors so we would not be disrupted. With keys in hand, Jean-Baptiste and Clément took us into the house for a much-anticipated look-around.

As we entered the house, we could see that it had not been lived in for some time and was stacked to capacity with antiques. There were wardrobes, statues, chests of drawers, grandfather clocks, an assortment of modern and antique desks. In truth, it was our first antique maize that we had ever had to navigate our way through, and we were enthralled.

We could, at a push, make out that the ground floor was in fact just one large room. Surprisingly, it looked to have been renovated in the 21st century because to the back of the room, in between all the various antiques, we spied a glossy fitted kitchen. As we looked downwards to the floor, we saw neutral and modern tiles. As we looked up, there were old beams running along the ceiling, but we could see that in between had been plastered and painted, and whilst keeping its old feel, the house looked to be in a good state.

I was craning my neck to peek behind a sizeable French antique wardrobe that had been placed to the back wall, but it wasn't fully up against the wall, and it was clear that there was a fireplace of some description behind it. It was impossible to find a way over to get a better look and I realised that I was going to have to be patient and wait until everything had been cleared out.

As we manoeuvred our way up the spiral staircase to the back of the house, we found ourselves again in a recently modernised space, housing two large double bedrooms and one bathroom which held a double sink, toilet and shower. It suited us three perfectly, other than the fact that we had hoped for a third bedroom where we could put up/accommodate visitors once we had settled in.

I knew from glancing over to Marc and Beth and seeing the look of happiness on their faces that they were pleased with the house and could imagine themselves living in it, as could I. I reached over to where Beth was standing, in what was to be her new bedroom – she could feel it as could I – and whispered into her ear to ask if she wanted to run down with me to the garden to check out the pool. Her face said it all as we ran down the stairs and out of the house hand in hand.

As we arrived down behind the dyke wall entangled with ivy, we stood literally staring at the most beautiful swimming pool we had ever seen. It was clear that there had been no budget when this pool had been created as it was lined in azure blue mosaic tiles with chrome ladders mounted to each end. To the top of the pool in the garden, one to each side, sat two large terracotta urns. To the right of the pool and centre to the pool sat a tall stone chimney which initially I took to be placed for ornamental purposes until I looked to the back of it to see an outdoor shower attached, which had long since corroded. Along the sides of the pool were placed various pieces of stonework, some with intricate carvings that stood to attention like gravestones almost, minus names. Beside the small stone pool house there stood a rather diseased-looking olive tree that had grown out of all proportion but added somewhat to the weird feeling of abandonment which filled me with excitement. As Beth and I walked between the pool and the large pine and oak trees that lined and protected the back of the property, we found a stack of old plastic garden furniture that had seen better days.

Like the garden described by Frances Hodgson Burnett, what made the garden utterly appealing was that this masterpiece had clearly been adored but for whatever reason had long since been abandoned. The grass looked to have been recently cut but it was clear that the creator of this beautiful garden had vanished, and the garden was crying out for the attention that it had once relished. In this grand pool sat rank water, and the azure mosaic tiles that lined the pool that would once have been sparkling were now layered with grime. Some of the tiles were missing and I got to thinking that if this pool could talk what would it tell Beth and I right now? Would it share with us stories about good times had by the family or did the current state of the pool suggest that there was a sad story to be told? Isn't it funny how we like to believe that inanimate objects at times can have feelings? If this pool did indeed have feelings, I was hoping that it was thrilled as it listened to Beth and I talk over all the work that we had in mind to restore it to its former glory.

Beth and I were sitting by the pool dangling our legs over the edge, each within our own world as we imagined what life could be like if we moved into this property. As we sat there daydreaming, we could hear the men walking over to us. I knew that we were all in agreement to take on the house, but I also knew that Marc was waiting for my confirmation and so when I saw him coming over, I jumped up and nodded for Marc to follow me so we could have a quiet chat.

"Marc, Beth and I love this garden and the pool is amazing, but we must do a deal that allows us to have use of each if we take on this house as the house itself with the terrace is not truly worth it." I looked up at Marc and hoped that the conversation with Clément and his father had gone well in the house and that there was some negotiating that could be done.

"Yes, I agree, this place suits us well until we find our own place. I will go over to them just now. Do you want to come over to join in or do you want me to do the negotiating?" he asked.

Just as I was about to respond to Marc, Clément walked over to us to ask if we wanted to go ahead with renting the house. As we both nodded in agreement, he surprised me with his next remark.

"Ah, that is good, but you…," he said, pointing at me. "…you must stay with your daughter as discussing money," he paused for effect, "in France, it is the business of men." I looked directly into his eyes and stayed focused for a moment. He had a look I had seen many times in my life. I kept eye contact for enough time to let him know that I was onto him and as I dropped eye contact, I casually wandered over to be with Beth. I had come up against this superior male attitude many times in my life and found it mentally exhausting.

Finally, the male huddle broke up and I could see by the face of each person that everyone looked to be happy with the outcome. As Marc walked over, he raised his thumb in the upwards position to let me know that we had negotiated the use of the pool and the garden. I was elated, as was Beth. A new chapter of our lives was about to commence.

With the assurance from Clément and Jean-Baptiste that our privacy would be respected with only Antoine living next door, we were eagerly looking forward to spending our first long hot summer in our new home as a family. The moving-in date was set for the 1st of April, which was around four weeks away and was intended to give the family the much-needed time to find a new home for the antiques currently being stored in the house.

Beth and I were pretty excited about moving in and having our pool, and Marc was…well, he was just Marc…happily looking forward to being settled.

Five

Our introduction to the French tribal family

We had opted to move into our new home over the course of two weeks, allowing time for Marc to give the place a fresh coat of paint and to collect and set up our furniture that had been sitting in storage.

One sunny but very cold morning, we had gone past the house to see how things were progressing and noticed that there were many people actively moving out furniture, so we decided to call in.

The gate was open, so we let ourselves in and walked down into the small front terrace. As we approached the front door of the house, we shouted in to say hello and hoped to see a face that we would recognise. We were instantly welcomed in by someone who was speaking in English and with a very good English accent, something that we had not anticipated. When we ventured into the living room, we traced the voice to an elderly lady who was sitting warming herself by the open fire.

"You must be Marc, Abi and Beth," she said as she slowly and carefully lifted herself out of her chair with one hand balanced on the chair. She gave us her other hand as she introduced herself.

"It is good to meet you all finally. I am Mia, the aged wife of Jean-Baptiste." She laughed and added, "Many years ago, I chose to marry a much younger man."

It was clear that she was very aware of the age difference between her and her husband. It was a noticeable difference that we guessed around ten to twelve years, made more obvious possibly with advancing years and declining health. Whilst we could see Jean-Baptiste helping to lift heavy items of furniture, Mia, we could see, was finding walking challenging, but it appeared that she still retained her youthful spirit and sense of humour.

"It is wonderful to meet you," I said. "Thank you so much for letting us rent your house."

Mia's face lit up. She was a fine-looking woman, with distinct hazel-coloured eyes and an almost perfect smile, let down only by teeth that had seen better days. She had a twinkle in her eyes, and I had a distinct feeling that this was going to be an interesting family to get to know.

I had the chance at this point to see the fireplace, which was previously hiding behind the antique wardrobe when we had first visited the house. With most of the furniture having been relocated, what was left behind was this ridiculously oversized stone fireplace that looked to have been taken out of a grand living room and for whatever reason someone had come up with the bizarre idea of installing it into this small space. Mia could see my interest in the fireplace and added:

"Do you like it, Abi? The fireplace dates to the eighteenth century. We had it installed many years ago but now I think it is far too big for this small space. What do you think?" she asked. I smiled as, for the first time in what felt like forever, I was going to have the opportunity to express myself in my own language rather than grasping for words in French and coming across as a very stupid foreigner.

"Yes, it is rather large," I replied, "but it is very different to what I am used to and for that reason alone I love it." I did my utmost to sound upbeat and grateful but as I looked around this very basic and compact space, I wondered if what was going through my head was similar to a monk as he gives up his Armani suit and picks up his itchy attire and walks for the first time into his sparsely furnished bedroom and thinks to himself, is this swap of material gain to a basic lifestyle going to be beneficial in any level to my inner soul? Time would tell.

There was a bundle of wood that had been placed into the fire grate and the fire was slowly starting to come alive, for which I was thankful, as the house was very cold. Mia looked to be frozen to the core despite wearing several layers of clothes finished off with a heavy red fleece.

"Antoine," Mia shouted and proceeded in French to utter what appeared to be an order and soon enough down the spiral stairs came this smallish man who looked to be no higher than 5ft. She spoke again and he hurried on outside and came back with an armful of firewood.

"It is too cold in this house, isn't it?" she asked us all. We all murmured our agreement.

"Have you met my son Antoine?" she asked as Antoine busily stacked the extra wood onto what was a rather miserable-looking fire at this stage, and as he completed his task, he picked up a small bottle and squirted it over the logs and the flames leapt up high into the chimney and the smoke came pouring out into the room, choking us all. The room erupted into laughter as we covered our eyes and reached out to shake hands with Antoine.

Antoine was very different in appearance to both Clément and his father, other than the common middle-aged distended stomach. He looked to be in his early fifties, with dark hair that was greying at the sides. He had a kind face, large eyes and a soft smile, and when he looked over to his mother his face took on the look of a little lost schoolboy. He was wearing a denim shirt with a black woollen waistcoat and a pair of denims. His shirt was unbuttoned on the low side, and nestled within his ample chest hair lay a gold medallion. He smelled strongly of aftershave and in his mouth was a cigarette that was hanging off the side of his lip, slowly smouldering, not such a great look but ultimately very French.

Marc at this stage had stepped outside to speak with Jean-Baptiste and was helping him to move some items of furniture into the awaiting van.

"It is good to have a chance to speak in English again. I do not often get the opportunity," Mia said as she directed the conversation to both Beth and I. "I hope that you are able to stay so that we can all have lunch together. In that way, we can all get to know each other."

"Of course, we would be more than happy to stay." I was speaking on Marc's behalf at this point and hoped he would be okay with it because I knew of no way to get out of the invitation without appearing rude. Beth was not a girl that embraced sudden decisions, so I quickly bent down to whisper in her ear.

"Don't worry, we will not stay too long, just something to eat and we will go home." Thankfully, she nodded in approval. "Your job is to go outside and to tell Dad of our new plans," I added, and with that she disappeared quickly outside as I could see that she was anxious to get away from all the oldies and have a run around the garden.

"How about you both…" Mia announced, pointing to Antoine and I. "…go over to the *boulangerie* to get some lunch for us all?" and with that she shouted further instructions to Antoine, who then raced over to give her her handbag, which had been sitting on a chest of drawers to the far end of the room.

Antoine and I looked at each other and then to Mia, who was holding out money for us to take as it appeared she was going to buy us all lunch. Antoine took the money and together we walked out of the house, out of the gate and across to the *boulangerie*.

It was a typical French *boulangerie* with the unusual option of being able to order chips as well as burgers, which were served in hot baguettes. Antoine seemed to fancy some hot food, so with the order put in, we awkwardly went about trying to have a conversation.

Antoine, it turned out, could speak a little English and with my small French vocabulary we managed to pass the time as we waited for our order to be called. It was as awkward as it sounds.

When we returned, Marc, Jean-Baptiste and Mia were all sitting around the fire and the conversation looked to be in full flow. As Antoine and I started to distribute lunch, I could hear Mia and Marc laughing and then Mia translating for Jean-Baptiste, who started to laugh also. It was all rather delightful.

We all munched through lunch trying desperately to find some heat near the fire, from which the heat, despite the amount of wood, looked to be vanishing up the chimney. It was a reality check, as I could see that the winter months might be a little challenging in this house. The good old days of setting the thermostat to 23 was soon going to be a distant memory. Thankfully, however, I did spot electric radiators in the bedrooms.

I liked Mia instantly. She was feisty and vivacious and when she spoke everyone jumped to her attention. I had never experienced a family such as this one as in both Marc's family and my own, no one was ever truly in control, and when you walked out of home, you were free to do as you so desired. This did not look to be the case in this instance, and I was fascinated by proceedings.

Mia and I were tuned in from the start, sharing the same sense of humour and laughing about ridiculous things. As we chatted, she occasionally barked orders, and I watched her husband and son time and time again jump to her attention. The startled look on my face as I glanced over to Marc for reassuring eye contact most likely asked for an explanation.

"In my family, Abi, my mother was the matriarch. She looked after us all until she died. Now it is my turn to be head of my family." She looked to have carved out for herself a chiefly role, even though her two boys had long since grown up. Having experienced the 'clan family' in Scotland, where it is common for the family member with the lowest self-esteem to control the family, ensuring that no one gets above their station (that's my take on it anyway), I wondered quietly to myself if this type of French family would be the same, as I had heard some horror stories about European mother-in-laws.

With lunch finished, we kept our promise to Beth and made our excuses to leave. We gave our word that we would see them all again soon and, of course, with the necessity of paying rent in cash each month, I was certainly going to be visiting Jean-Baptiste and Mia on a regular basis. Everyone seemed friendly, welcoming and genuinely glad to meet us, which was endearing, and I was looking forward to getting to know Mia better. I had so many questions to ask her, mainly related to life in France during the occupation of the Germans and how this had affected her family and her as a person. It was clear that she was a lady who, like Antoine, was eager to speak to new people, and she seemed more than happy to recount stories of her life in her younger years as we conversed during lunch. I had a good feeling about this family.

On the 1st of April, the house was ready for Beth and I to move into. Unfortunately, due to a depletion of monetary funds, Marc had no option but to accept a couple of jobs back in Scotland for clients he had worked for previously. It was less than ideal but Marc planned to come home as often as he could and prior to leaving had all the furniture and boxes in place, so it was a matter of Beth and I emptying the boxes and creating ourselves a family home.

Antoine had come over on several occasions to speak with me to pass the time of day. At first, he appeared extremely nervous, and I tried my utmost to make him feel comfortable with the offer of beer and chatting about daily events. He would often speak to me about his brother and explained that he wasn't his full brother but his half-brother, and that Jean-Baptiste was not his father but only the father of Clément. I guess he was trying to distance himself from these two and I was keen to find out why.

"My brother, he is crazy." was a statement that he attached to any story where his brother made an appearance. His index finger would reach up to his temple as he spun it around to ensure I knew that Clément had some issues, although I wondered if it was just sibling rivalry.

Clément too had been calling in to see me several times per week after he finished work, under the guise of checking in on Beth and I on account of Marc not being present. He always seemed to be in a hurry, stopping for a quick beer before scurrying off home. "I am not in good relations with my brother," he was keen to tell me, explaining, "He is not my brother. He is not the son of my father, only of my mother. My brother, he is crazy." Like Antoine when he mentioned his brother, he shook his head in despair.

One afternoon I was busy in the garden whilst Beth was at school, planting flower seeds in some large terracotta pots that I had purchased in order to make the front terrace pretty for the forthcoming summer months. I looked up, as I could smell the strong mix of cigarettes and aftershave and knew that Antoine was making his way over for post-lunch coffee. He was looking very emotional and, sure enough, as he sat with me by the table in the warm sunshine, he confessed.

"I am happy, very much, to have people beside me." His eyebrows were knitted together; his large brown eyes looked quite teary as he placed his hand on his chest. "I live here only me. I do not have many friends. It is good to talk to someone." When he had finished speaking, he smiled across at me in a manner that was almost childlike. I got the distinct impression that this was one very lonely man. I reached out to rest my hand on his arm as I assured him that I too was happy to have him as our neighbour.

As Antoine relaxed in my company on his regular visits, he was keen to show me around. There was not only our house and Antoine's, but in between both of our houses existed a third part that, fortunately for us, was uninhabited. From the front of this expansive property looking from the roadside, it looked to have originally been built as a three-storey farmhouse, which Antoine was living in, and gradually over the years other parts were added on for workers maybe or family members, such as the part we were now renting. Neither Mia nor Antoine could fill me in on the history of it as Mia had purchased the house in sections when it had been completely dilapidated. I was super keen to have a look around to see what was inside this building, but I had more than a sneaky suspicion that I was going to be greeted by stacks of French antiques, if what had been stored in our house was anything to go by.

When Antoine huffed and puffed and finally managed to open the large old wooden double doors, I found myself standing for what seemed like an age as I took in what was presented to me. I recalled the TV show *American Pickers* that Marc used to watch back in the UK and thought of his excitement when he finally returned home as it was likely he was going to be rummaging around this space for hours.

This was a room with high ceilings where every wall was lined with metal racking and on each shelf there were hundreds of plastic boxes containing every conceivable item you could possibly collect in several lifetimes, such as door handles, door knockers, rusted tins of screws, nails, books, musical instruments, wickerware, old pots and pans, clocks, old French toys, Meccano sets, tin signs, film memorabilia – to include a life-size cardboard cut-out of Indiana Jones perched against a wall – various coffee grinders, rusting cookware, wood and metal working tools, etc. On another wall, the racking looked to house a stack of coffins. The clue as to what these were lay on the clock faces that were hung above the shelving. These were dismantled grandfather and grandmother clocks. Later, we would learn from Clément that Jean-Baptiste thought that it would be a good idea to start a collection when the clocks had dropped in value, to hang onto them and sell when the prices had climbed, but that never seemed to have materialized and these beautiful clocks remained stacked in position.

In the centre of the room there were the typically large bulky French wardrobes and sideboards, many of which had long since gone out of fashion due to, I would imagine, the dramatically reduced size of the modern French family home. Walking through to an adjacent room, there was a collection of kitchen dressers dating from the 1920s to the 1950s. These would have been common at one time within every kitchen in France but with the, albeit late, arrival of modern kitchens into many French homes, it was likely that there were still thousands of similar old dressers in circulation.

It was difficult to manoeuvre through each room as there were boxes and various tools stacked on the floor, making it difficult to avoid tripping. There was so much to take your attention that I had to make a concerted effort to tell myself to look down. As we walked deeper into what felt like an unending space, I spied a secondary floor that looked only to be accessible by extension ladders. There were large sections of the floor missing so it was easy enough just to look up and see hundreds of old wooden dining chairs stacked haphazardly on top of each other and stacked onto old upholstered chairs. Everything looked centuries old, apart from the modern five-piece drum set I could see crammed into a corner. When I looked at the extension ladders, I couldn't help but wonder how on earth they managed to get these items up there.

This space just kept giving, as Antoine pushed open a second set of double wooden doors that led us into an area that had a very different feel to it as to the left was an impressive stone walk-in fireplace that took me by surprise as it was certainly not original in this farm style of house and was far more suited to a château. There were so many questions I wanted to ask Antoine but with the language barrier I found myself increasingly struck dumb and found it easier just to ooh and aah at what I hoped were the right moments. As I followed Antoine through each space, I could see that I was providing him with the correct reaction, and he was lapping it up. This was a special room, Antoine explained to me in English, as he wore what I considered a very proud smile; a room, he continued, where his family stored their treasured possessions bequeathed to them from family members who had long since passed away. He pointed out various armoires, and an exquisite wooden inlaid dining table and chairs that had been inherited by Mia from her mother. I opened the door to one of the armoires to peek inside and spotted a beautiful blue and white dinner service, which Antoine informed me had again belonged to Mia's mother. Antoine went onto explain that whilst these items had substantial monetary value, the family valued them for who had owned them, and these items were never to be sold. They would just continue to sit there, I guessed, until Mia and Jean-Baptiste had passed on. So far, from knowing these two brothers for such a short amount of time, I noticed that most of their sentences started or finished with, "when my parents die."

To the back of the room were stacked what looked to be hundreds of archived-sized boxes, which Antoine said were a combination of unsold items from when his parents had owned the antique shop, and further bits and pieces inherited from relatives. In amongst all of this sat broken chairs, tables with legs missing, cracked vases, broken lampshades and light fittings with many parts presumed lost. On shelves there sat damaged ornaments and stacks of paintings from dead relatives, and I started to wonder if this family ever threw anything out. Under a mountain of old blankets and curtains I could see what looked to be an adult-sized pram. What on earth was this? Antoine explained that quite correctly it was designed for adults as it was around 6ft in length, and was used to take sick people to Lourdes. Behind the pram, I could just about make out wine racks running along the full length of the room. This was far more interesting than the pram.

"My late uncle gave me his wine and champagne collection," Antoine said as he followed my eyes locating the wine. As he told me this, I could see his chest puffing out, which gave me the impression that he had enjoyed a close relationship with his uncle and was considerably proud to have been chosen by him to receive his collection.

I wondered if the wine and champagne had any value, though, stacked into this space. As we got closer, he picked up a bottle and showed me the label dated 1951 and another, 1959, but both bottles were in a terrible state with perished corks. These bottles, sure enough, were stored on their sides and in a dark, dry area, but I knew no more than that about storing wine. Looking at Antoine's face, with his eyes lit up and a proud smile, I could see that the value was of no concern. This was his collection and I doubted it was going anywhere.

I was desperate for Marc to come home to see all of this. As for Beth, she had run into the large space, shouted to find me and declared when I got home that it was the biggest pile of junk she had ever seen!

Mia and Jean-Baptiste lived around twenty minutes from our house, in a village a lot bigger than the one we were living in. Whilst built in the centre of the village, their house was not the typical narrow three-storey mid-terrace townhouse but instead a large two-storey house, attached to their neighbour at one end and detached at the other. It also had its own driveway and front garden. They had opted for white shutters with matching coloured railings and gates that secured their house and driveway. On the paved pathway leading up to the front door had been set a high arched canopy with an exquisite selection of roses that entangled their way from the soil bed up and over the canopy. It was a beautiful sight to behold when the roses were in full bloom.

Exiting the rose canopy took me up a set of stairs and up to their front door, which looked to be on the first floor, making me wonder what was on the ground floor. The first time that I entered their home and with introductions complete, I couldn't help but feel that I had walked into an antique shop. The first floor was a large open space with a living area to one side, dining room in the centre and a wooden fitted kitchen with kitchen table to the far side. There was so much to see that I asked Mia if she wouldn't mind giving me a tour. I felt that this would make her happy as I could clearly see that she had surrounded herself with treasured possessions and I was keen to hear the history behind each item.

In the living area and positioned high above their antique pink marble carved fire surround hung a large oil painting of a fine-looking lady, maybe in her forties, dressed in a long, flowing deep-red taffeta ruffled gown. Around her neck sat a diamond necklace and styled into her chestnut-coloured hair, she wore a wide-brimmed hat with flowers. With her hands clasped together neatly on her lap, it was a picture that indicated a privileged lifestyle of someone who lived in the early twentieth century.

"This picture you are looking at, Abi, is an oil portrait of my mother when she was seeing a count who insisted that he had a picture of her commissioned to hang in his study. Isn't my mother beautiful?" Mia was standing with me as she held onto the back of the sofa and was clearly mesmerised, as I was, by this beautiful lady that sat before us.

"My mother had a difficult life initially after having me, but because she was beautiful it was not difficult for her to attract rich men and whilst at times these men were hard to please and often had several mistresses other than herself, it did allow her to take pleasure in a lifestyle that was not always experienced by other ladies at her age at this time in France," Mia explained, and she added, "I think it is better that I have my husband show you around the rest of the house as it is too difficult for me now." And with that she shouted for her husband, who came through from another room into the living area to take his instructions from his wife.

As Mia continued to hold onto the sofa for support, she explained that most of the items of furniture that were placed in the living and dining area had belonged to her mother, and with being an only child, she had gone onto inherit everything from her mother as well as from her grandmother. She continued that it was due to her inheritance that she was able to buy the house that Antoine was now living in, and as other parts of the property came up for sale, she was gradually able to purchase the whole building and the garden plots that came with them. Her inheritance she said was life changing.

I used what was becoming my new skill of oohing and aahing at the appropriate occasions as Mia and Jean-Baptiste spoke to me about the host of curios that decorated their beautiful home. From the dancing blue ceramic elephant that sat proudly on an exquisite walnut hall table to the oil painting of a crying clown that was hung by the dining table, giving the area a rather melancholy feel. The dining table and carved dining chairs with leather upholstery were early nineteenth century, Mia explained, and gifted to her by an uncle. By the front door I noticed an aerial photo of the house that we had just moved into and how different it was now to when this was taken. Mia was following my eyes and when my eyes landed on the photo, she explained that when the photograph had been taken, they had only just finished renovating the main part of the farmhouse that Antoine was now living in. The swimming pool had just been installed but there was no garden as such surrounding it as she had yet to have this designed. The aerial photograph showed the extensive farmhouse with the outbuildings and the swimming pool surrounded only by fields. I now knew who was behind the design of this charming garden and I intended to speak to her about this on another visit.

The tour of the house surprised me with a fully renovated modern bathroom with twin sinks above which sat a striking arch-shaped mirror with a wide black metal frame where horses leapt and bounded from one side to the other. I had never seen anything like it in my life. Mia shouted through from the living area to the bathroom to explain to me that she had found this mirror when she was travelling many years ago and had spent every *franc* she had on it in order to ship it back home. I thought to myself that I would certainly have done the same if I had ever found this mirror for sale. Mia certainly had a good eye for fine things and was sure to purchase anything that she fell in love with, which looked to have happened countless times in her life.

Mia was keen to walk through with Jean-Baptiste when it came to showing me her bedroom. Their bedroom was a considerable size, with five large windows looking down over the garden. Aqua-blue velvet curtains hung from a covered embroidered pelmet from the top of the high ceiling, draping prettily down to the floor. Each curtain had an embroidered tie-back to match the pelmet. It was a bedroom fit for royalty. A large wooden bed with a tapestry headboard and above it hung a gold cherub playing the trumpet. There were many beautiful antique pieces such as the small writing bureau with carved chair positioned by a door that led down into the garden. It was a gorgeous spot and with the sun's rays projected onto this area and with the number of letters that were stacked onto the desk, as well as a book that sat open, I could see that this was a favoured area for Mia to sit during the long days. A round pedestal table inlaid with a contrasting design sitting to the centre of the room with two chairs quilted with a fabric similar in style to the pelmet looked likely to be where Mia enjoyed her morning coffee.

"Sit for a moment, Abi, and I will introduce you to all of my family," Mia instructed as I obediently sat down on one of her chairs.

With the help of her husband, together they gathered up the photographs they had on display on each of the chest of drawers and tables as well as those that hung loosely on the walls surrounding her bed. The first photo that was handed to me was in black and white and was of a beautiful young lady who must have been in her early to mid-twenties, sitting on a chair in the middle of a garden, smiling at the camera. She was wearing a short-sleeved fitted blouse and what looked to be a pencil skirt, and her hair was in a neat bob.

"Can you guess who this is?" Mia asked me, but her smile gave it away.

I looked closely at the photograph and sure enough I could see the similarity as I regarded the eyes of the young lady and of this elderly lady who now sat across from me.

"My guess is that it is you," I replied.

"Yes, it is me. Some people used to say that I resembled Katherine Hepburn." She paused before continuing in a very sad tone. "I used to be very beautiful but now I am just an old lady."

"You looked very much like Katherine Hepburn," I assured her as I glanced back at the photo and back to Mia, "and you still have your beautiful eyes that sparkle and your sense of humour that I guess you had at that young age." It was as much as I could come up with as I got a feeling that this was a lady who had thoroughly enjoyed being beautiful and was still coming to terms with having lost her youth despite being in her early eighties.

One by one, I was introduced to Mia's family, starting with her father and then onto her mother, who I noted were never in the same photograph, then onto her grandparents, aunts, cousins and her own children, with some more modern pictures of her grandchildren. It was evident from how handsome her father had been and how beautiful her mother had been where Mia had gained her good looks.

Mia was clearly fond of her father and proud of how handsome he was, but she became sad when she spoke about him leaving her mother when she was around ten years of age. He had gone onto have a child with his next lady, and no sooner had their child been born than he was off with lady number four. Another child was born and I kind of got a bit lost in the story at this point as to what happened thereafter. Mia therefore had three step-siblings, two of whom were still alive and one of whom she spoke to several times a week. Her father seemed to have been well connected with various government departments which looked to have allowed him an income to at least financially support his offspring. I found it unusual as Mia spoke about her childhood that her mother had contacted each of his mistresses to ensure that all his children had the opportunity to know each other. In this way, the mothers created their own family, giving Mia three brothers. Mia had such sadness in her eyes when she spoke of her father, and I felt that there was a lot more to this story than she wished to let on. Her way of dealing with the sadness of her childhood appeared to be by sharing the few stories she remembered of her father being part of her life, and of those there didn't appear to be many.

A photo of what was clearly Antoine and Clément playing in someone's garden in faded colour was passed over to me next.

"I love this photo, Abi, but, my boys, they fight for my attention. They have a bad relation, and it makes life very difficult for my husband and I." She sighed as she held onto what appeared to be a very precious photograph and maybe, by the looks of it, the only one in existence where her two boys appeared to be playing together happily.

"I am not welcome at the house of Clément. His wife, she is a peasant girl. She has never stepped foot in my house. She invites us for Christmas lunch each year but that is all. Once we have lunch, we play a few games of cards and then we leave until we are invited back the following Christmas. She does not have a good relation with my husband. He does not like our son being married to a peasant and she knows that well."

As I sat with Mia, I pondered over everything that I had been told thus far by each member of her family and I thought how sad it was that within such a small family there were so many disagreements.

Appearing keen to get to know us, Antoine and Clément regularly called in, and as we stopped what we were doing, quickly getting our brains into French mode, we would listen to all their woes about their family, and these seemed to be endless. Like Mia, they did not hold back on sharing their feelings towards each other. We had only lived in their rental for just over four weeks and yet we knew so much about the faults and shortcomings of each member of this family. In truth, it was starting to become a little wearisome. I was desperate for Marc to come home so I could live within the realms of my own family and not theirs.

That afternoon, I cut short the conversation, made my excuses to leave to collect Beth and drove back home. I needed time to think about all of this. We had found ourselves becoming embroiled in something that was none of our business, the life of another family whose existence until recently we had never known of. Each member of this family seemed to need to talk to someone outside the family, and yet by telling us of their woes, what did they hope to gain? Was this just normal French family life or was it something more? Having just landed on these shores, and with neither Marc nor I coming from a tribal family, we hadn't a clue what was going on.

Six

Preparing for our first long hot summer

I remember a line in the endearing and brilliant film set in Italy entitled *Call Me by Your Name*, directed by Luca Guadagnino, when the American guest asked the Italian mother, "What do you do in the long hot Italian summers?" and the response was along the lines of, "Wait until the long hot summer comes to an end." Which was followed by, "What do you do after that when winter arrives?" and my favourite-ever response was "Why, wait of course for the long hot summer to start again." This film had not yet been released when we were about to commence our first French summer as residents, but it was a part of the film that rung true with each of us and a clear explanation to family and friends as to why we upped and moved to the South of France.

It was now the middle of May. The news from Marc that he was planning to come home was a godsend as I was finding daily life far more stressful than I had ever anticipated. Between school runs, homework, my own work, paying tax on time, learning French and at times feeling overwhelmingly lonely, and it did not help when I found a Frenchman on my doorstep, having arrived unannounced. As friendly as these two brothers appeared to be, I would have preferred to have been left to my own devices as these two seemed intent on telling me how to live and to extract every detail about how I was living so they could share this amongst the family. Surely their lives were not that boring. But it appeared that they were. Talking to my neighbours back in the UK was a joy as I didn't have to plan what I was going to say, as words flow freely when you speak the same lingo, but here I had to make a concerted effort to plan everything I wished to say using my limited French, added to that what was coming out of their mouths sounded nothing like the French I had learnt at school, and there was always Clément's little snide sexist remarks to deal with.

I was lying back in the garden on a sun lounger one Friday afternoon, in dream land, when Antoine called around to ask if I would like to come over that evening for an *apero* so that he could introduce me to a couple of his friends. It was just what I needed and without having to think about a response, I jumped at the opportunity and suggested that I could bring some food to share for an evening meal. This was also to his liking and very quickly I had a night out planned which meant a simple case of stepping out of my front door and walking down to the back of the garden and to the right, which would take me into Antoine's back terrace. I had planned to enjoy a couple of drinks without having to worry about finding my way back home. I now had to explain my decision to my darling nine-year-old, whose idea of an evening out was certainly not sitting at a table with four adults over drinks.

Beth and I had cut a deal; she was to politely meet our new acquaintances and to sit down for one soft drink. Once she had finished her drink, and it was up to her how quickly she wished to drink it, she was allowed to excuse herself politely and slip out to play in the garden. When our meal was ready, I would call for her and she would be able to eat with us what she wished with the promise that if she did not like anything I would make her toasties when we returned home. We shook on it.

At 7pm, Beth and I nervously walked over to Antoine's back garden, each carrying plates containing chicken salad, roast potatoes and a bottle of wine. This was the first time that I had ventured over to see Antoine and despite the size of the shared garden that backed onto both of our houses, he too had a small terrace to the back of his house, but unlike mine it was paved and furnished with various antiquities. Guests, I could see, had yet to arrive, so once I had placed the food on the outside table, allowing Antoine to ferry it into his kitchen to place in the fridge, I asked him to enlighten me as to the use of one item that had caught my eye. It was a long rectangular wooden rack, with three large holes that contained three large clay jugs. The rack was supported by a roughly sawn base.

"This is a Spanish antique," Antoine informed me. "It was used many years ago to store water or wine and it would have been kept in the house rather than outside in the garden. Do you like it?" he asked.

"I love it," I said honestly, because whilst it was a much-needed conversation piece and I was always desperately looking for and thinking up something, it was also a beautiful item, especially as to the back of it he had a large flowerbed built up to waist height that took up two sides of this terrace, and in these beds sat a gorgeous mixture of flowers in full bloom which gave the terrace a wonderful ambiance. It may have given his garden a beautiful smell too, but with the strong smell of cigarettes and aftershave, it wasn't likely that anything else could reach one's nostrils.

In the middle of the terrace sat a large metal table with a ceramic tiled top and eight ornate chairs to match. I was wondering if Antoine had created this beautiful space or whether it was another area designed by his mother. Beth and I sat down and smiled at each other. It was clear by her expression that she was bored already, and we had only just arrived, so I was hoping that there would be an offer of drinks without waiting for any guests.

"Would you care for a *kir*, Abi?" Antoine said as he popped his head around his kitchen door.

"What is it?" I asked as in truth whilst I had heard of the drink, I wasn't really one for mixing drinks, so I did not know what it was. A G&T or a glass of wine was my normal tipple.

"It is a drink that we French like to serve often for an *apero*. It is a French blackcurrant liquor mixed with white wine. Does that sound okay?" he asked. "It is good, I promise."

"Perfect," I replied.

"Coca for you, Beth?" he asked.

"*Eau, s'il vous plaît*," replied Beth. I was a very proud mummy when I heard her speak in French. For a reason unbeknown to either Marc or myself, Beth had made a promise to herself a few years previously to never drink Coca-Cola and she was now nine and had kept it. When anyone ever asked her if she would like a Coke or, as we were finding was common in France, *Coca*, she would always wrinkle up her nose and put on a face of disgust that we would often have to explain. Fortunately, this evening, she was clear about what she wanted to drink, and it was promptly served.

I had just taken a quick sip of my *kir* and was about to announce to Antoine that it was indeed lovely when the doorbell rang. I heard the usual greetings and bisous, followed a few minutes later by Antoine coming out into the terrace to introduce his friend.

"Abi, this is my longtime friend Asad," he announced.

Beth and I shook hands with Asad as he sat down with me to enjoy a beer which Antoine had pre-empted and placed on the table alongside a couple of bowls of crisps.

Beth held up her empty glass to show me that she had finished her water in record time, and I nodded my approval for her to run off and play.

Asad was a lot younger than Antoine and I guessed around thirty years of age. He was around 6ft and of slim build, olive-skinned, handsome with large brown eyes, good teeth and a charming smile, and he exuded confidence.

Asad explained that it had been some time since he had spoken English but with the arrival of our second round of drinks, my French was on the up as was his English, and between the three of us we were able to have a laugh about many a subject. The doorbell rang again and with a slightly longer wait for introductions, following Antoine out to the terrace came this beautiful lady, I guessed a little younger than myself in her early forties. He introduced her as his new friend Camille. She had shoulder-length brown hair with a slight curl, green eyes, a slight hint of make-up and she was wearing very tight-fitting trousers that must have been around a size 6, with a pretty, flower-patterned blouse tucked in loosely. I had arrived feeling quite slim in my size 10 shorts but now I was starting to feel on the fat side, such was her delicate frame. She towered above Antoine, but we all did.

Camille had arrived a little later than planned and I sensed that she was a little distressed. I had never met her before so this could have been her usual demeanor, but Antoine too looked concerned for her and was fussing about her until she asked him to leave her as she insisted that she would feel better after a few drinks and a cigarette. With that, she sat down and reaching into her handbag she pulled out a packet of Philip Morris and leaned over to offer each of us a cigarette. Asad took advantage of her offer, as did Antoine, although his signature smoldering cigarette to the side of his mouth was ever-present. As the small garden terrace began to fill with smoke, I was glad that Beth was out in the garden playing. I was used to living in a society whereby people asked for the approval of their guests before lighting up, and even in the UK this was a long time coming. I had no plans to make a fuss that evening, but I did make the decision to make a point of stopping this from happening in my own garden, as Clément and Antoine had no hesitation in planting themselves at our garden table, lighting up and blowing their smoke in our faces.

Antoine had cooked up a few steaks on the BBQ and with the addition of the food that Beth and I had brought over, we all enjoyed a lovely evening, especially when we had moved onto a glass or three of local red wine. Beth had made sure to eat her meal in supersonic time and was back out playing in the garden and had discovered to her delight that Antoine owned a cat.

The highlight of the evening was Asad asking us if we cared to see his impression of a snail. This was made funnier by Antoine insisting that we saw Asad's snail because it was worth seeing and incredibly funny to watch. Camille looked at me with a rather startled face and I could see that she was likely to be thinking what I was thinking…was Asad planning to drop his trousers? Camille and I started to laugh and the more we thought about the question, the more we laughed until finally Antoine and Asad cottoned on to why we were both laughing so hard and assured us that it was an actual impression and not one that involved the removal of trousers. Phew!

Asad's impression of a snail went along like this. He took several moments to get himself into position as he sat at the table and waited for the laughter to stop. Slowly, he lowered his head down into his chest, staying like that for effect, and very slowly he lifted his head to show a contorted face. He slowly moved his head to look at us all one by one. Gone were his good looks as his eyes narrowed, and his mouth bulged and moved around as if he was chomping on a large piece of chewing gum. As he slowly raised his head, he started to speak in what I guess he thought was the accent of a snail. It was ridiculous but very entertaining.

As the evening went on, Camille started to speak to us about her life and how she had been a mistress to a Frenchman and had waited patiently for many years for him to leave his wife to allow them to be together. Finally, he either confessed to having no intention of leaving his wife or it slowly dawned on her that she was being led a merry dance and they had split up. She explained that she had given him everything and had received nothing. She had left it too late to have children and she was back living with her mother. This may have been the reason behind her low mood, as she was keen to speak about it.

I liked Asad and Camille. They seemed good people and I decided the following weekend, with Marc driving home accompanied by one of his friends, to invite everyone around for Sunday lunch. Camille at this stage was only a maybe and Asad said that he would ask his fiancée, who was now also invited. I wanted Marc to be a part of this.

Marc arrived back home the following Monday with his friend John in tow. Marc had been gone for just over five weeks and it was a delight to be all together again, with the bonus of having our first visitor.

It was hotter than either Marc or John had envisaged, and I could see that they were both struggling at times with the temperature. There was also the unexpected problem of flies.

The word *problem* is far too weak a word to describe the intolerable level of flies that were hatching. In front of the word *problem* in this instance rests the word *gargantuan*.

As the weather heated up towards the end of April, Beth and I were killing around seventy to eighty flies each morning when we came downstairs for breakfast. We would each grab a fly swat and run around the open living space from the kitchen to the front door killing every fly that was landing on the windows and furniture, and when we looked up, they were also crawling along the beams. It was ghastly!

Sitting outside under the tree for lunch and our evening meals, and things on the fly side were no better. I was hoping

Marc would have some ideas as to what to do when he returned home. He was used to flies growing up in New Zealand to the point that he had made fly screens for each of the windows and doors at his parents' house to stop the flies from entering.

Marc was aghast at the number of flies within the house and garden and said that whilst in New Zealand flies could be bothersome, he had never seen anything like it. Where were they hatching? As there were so many walking along the ceiling beams, we could only think that it was from this location, so with windows and doors open we spent several hours carefully spraying this area and hoped to God for a breakthrough. We had fly tape up beside the door and at various positions throughout the house and garden. We purchased numerous fly swats as, with so many flies being obliterated each day, they were not lasting past a week, with pieces breaking and flying off with every whack. As we were in and out of the house all day long, we opted to put up a light linen curtain at the doorway in case flies were coming in. It was a little better but not great.

What a busy week that turned out to be as summer came racing towards us and the pool had yet to be cleaned. With the size of this pool, I presumed it would take several weeks to heat up, but there was that part of me who thought if I remained positive and hopeful it would take a lot less.

The biggest problem facing us (I refer to *us* as Marc and I had drafted in John and Antoine) was the stubborn grime that was ingrained into the tiles. It was almost as if they had been coated with a thin layer of Artex, and most British people in the early '90s knew all too well how difficult this was to get removed from their homes when it went quickly out of fashion.

It turned out the Artex was calcium and we had noticed since moving into our house that the calcium build-up in the kettle was to the point where I was brushing the kettle out most days with a stainless-steel cleaning ball or else small clumps of calcium were being poured into tea or when cooking rice or pasta, etc. By the looks of things, it had been several years since the pool had been used, and the calcium had become baked onto the tiles by the hot sun.

We each tried scrubbing the tiles with various implements, which seemed to be either doing nothing or they were too sharp leaving scratch marks behind. Finally, we found in the supermarkets a strong enough acid that removed the calcium, but there were two problems. The first was that it was overpowering in its smell as well as burning the skin, which meant trying to find an old pair of trousers and an old long-sleeved tee-shirt, face mask and gloves, which were all difficult to wear in the heat. Secondly, it was taking such a long time to clean small sections of mosaic. Decisions had to be made. A lot of beer was drunk that hot afternoon as we each stood inside the pool, sweating profusely, looking around as we discussed how far we were all prepared to take this cleaning job.

Finally, the decision was made to get buckets of hot soapy water. Each with a scrubbing brush, we would wash down the walls and the floors as best we could, get out the hose, wash it down, use the water pump to empty all the dirty water and hopefully by that stage we could look at filling up the pool. It was too hot to be larking around wasting time.

That's exactly what we did and within three days of starting our epic renovation project, the pool was clean, by our joint standards anyway, and the water sat glistening and hopefully warming up under the baking sun. It was still May and yet it was hot, very hot indeed.

A bonus to this pool was that prior to having it installed, the family had paid for a man to come out who was experienced at using divining rods and, sure enough, he found an underground spring, which I gather became the location for the swimming pool. With pipes and a pump installed into the pool house, it made it a lot easier to top the pool up, plus there was no cost attached to it thereafter. Was it legal? No idea.

Sunday lunch went ahead as scheduled on our large farmhouse table that we had taken from our dining space and swapped with the smaller table that we normally used to ensure we all had plenty of space as we sat under the shade of the tree on our front terrace. I was a little hesitant about preparing French food because it was doubtful that it would reach French standards, so instead, I opted to cook Greek. Greek feta and spinach pies for *entrée* with a small serving of tzatziki, moussaka and salad for our *plat principal* and for *le dessert* I simply walked across to our village *boulangerie* and bought a gateau (28€, ouch).

Asad arrived with his delightful and beautiful fiancée Emma. Antoine walked over with his signature cigarette and a spare packet to ensure he did not run out. Camille was a no-show. After seeing the longing in Antoine's eyes when he spoke with her previously, it was not a shock that she did not turn up. She had accepted an invitation to a restaurant with him prior to us all meeting together, but a third acceptance was going to lead this man on. He had confessed to me that he had high hopes for a relationship with Camille, and whilst I did not wish to appear unkind and state that she was a good bit above his station, I did mention that maybe a rebound relationship was not such a good idea after such a toxic break-up, to which he agreed.

To our delight, Emma could speak English very well as she was a trained English teacher, and so as fortune would have it, we again had a translator in our midst that allowed us all to speak freely. I remember that afternoon setting out my beautiful etched wine glasses that my sister had bought for me as a gift a few years earlier, and glasses that I had taken very good care of. A phenomenon to which I was unfortunately to become accustomed, the southerly wind referred to by the locals as the *mistral* can hit out of the blue, as it did this hot sunny afternoon, lifting my beautiful glasses quickly into the air and smashing them back down onto the table. Did I learn my lesson when I entertained after that? Nope, and by the end of our first summer all my good glasses were in smithereens and on the table sat everyday glasses purchased at the local supermarket. It was no wonder that the French spoke of the *mistral* sending them crazy!

Seven

You give them a hand...

"*Tu donnes la main, ils prennent le bras*" is a common French expression relating to people who take advantage of generosity. It translates into English as *You give them a hand and they take the whole arm*. This chapter encompasses many of these types of people. I have only noted the first part of the saying in the heading of this chapter because the French have a unique way of pushing their luck, which has created two chapters in this book.

It was mid-June and Marc was still home. We had a small budget which was mostly going on house rent, school fees and food shops. Food was very expensive compared to the UK. Shop-bought gateaux and restaurant meals had been put on hold as we worked out how to find Marc employment.

With the occasional light bulb going off and a lot of clockwork noises, sighs of despair, no light at the end of the tunnel, then a possible crack of light at the end of the tunnel, we can thank wine and sunshine for allowing us to cope with our situation which at this stage was at crisis point.

The pool had heated up and within the first week of using the pool, Beth had taught herself to swim. I could not believe my eyes when I saw her take off and swim up to the deep end without any swimming aides. She had been taking swimming lessons back in the UK but she was always a little put off when children in her class would dive in and swim with ease from the shallow end to the deep, and with the insecurity children often feel at this age, it was debilitating her efforts. I could clearly see that lessons were not a waste of time as she had learnt to swim in her head and needed only a quiet pool in which to experiment.

It was so quiet and peaceful, albeit the traffic noise from the road that went by our house, but we were becoming accustomed to that, and it was really only busy with morning and evening work traffic. We swam first thing before breakfast and spent our long hot afternoons practising diving and water aerobics, and Beth and I had purchased every conceivable blow-up imaginable to include giant lobsters, crocodiles, a whale and numerous water loungers in the shape of lollipops, pizza slices, etc. Antoine would regularly come over to have a beer with us when he had finished work, and we sat by the pool discussing the day's events and often sorting out the events of the world as you do after a few beers. Antoine would often comment about how cold the pool was and that he would not consider going into it until August, when it was just right. We had expected him to use it but have to say we were happier when he found the pool cold, as we were each enjoying spending time together as a family.

One evening, as Marc and I sat by the pool enjoying a glass of rosé, Marc said that whilst searching the internet for possible job ideas, he had found someone advertising for joiners on the UK Gumtree to work in the French Alps. At this stage, he wasn't sure of the exact location and how far he would be from us, and we sat deliberating the pros and cons. We could not up and leave Provence at this early stage, especially when Beth had just settled into school, so Marc decided that the best approach would be to simply respond to the advert and take it from there.

Three emails and numerous calls to a French-based mobile and Marc was losing hope. Was it a fake advert? He decided to give it one last shot and left a message stating that he was living in France, had his own van and tools and was ready to start work within the week. Within ten minutes he received a call from a man who apologised for ignoring his attempts at communication, explaining that his advert had attracted a lot of time-wasters. Marc was asked if he could start straight away, and the next day, Marc was packed up and gone.

It was back to just Beth and I each day and with the school holidays having started, we were enjoying some very lazy summer days. One of these afternoons at the start of July, as we walked over to the pool, we could see that someone was already in it. She looked to be in her late teens but who was she? I had never seen her before. I was a little startled by having someone I did not know in the garden, and I had expected Antoine to give me a heads-up if he was planning to invite anyone. We had never spoken about other people using the pool as when we took the house on, despite Antoine not being present in the discussions, we had been assured that we would have the pool and garden to ourselves.

I entered the pool, which by this point felt like I was entering a public pool.

"Bonjour," I said.

"Bonjour," she replied.

I did not know enough French to put together a sentence that would allow me to know who she was and why she was using the pool, and even if I did find enough words, I doubted I would have been able to understand her explanation, so I had no choice but to leave it.

That evening, as Antoine came sauntering over, having finally ditched his long-sleeved denim shirt and swapping it for a short-sleeved cream linen shirt, with his denims on (still no shorts), smoking the inevitable, to have a couple of beers, I thought I'd better ask who she was.

"Ah, it is Chloé, she is the daughter of Audrey, the lady that cleans my house," he responded sharply and added, "Audrey said it would be a good idea for her two daughters to come over to swim with Beth."

You did not think to ask me? I thought.

Beth needed company her own age, there was no doubt, but there was that other part of me that felt that perhaps Beth was just an excuse to wangle an invite for her daughters to spend their school holidays in our garden.

"Her other daughter, Manon, is closer to Beth's age, and she is coming over tomorrow for a swim. We think it would be a good idea for Beth," he added to my surprise.

I felt a little out of control at this point as I was not used to people making decisions on our behalf without consulting with us first.

I presented the external decision making out to Beth that it was my idea as in this way she would be more willing to buy into it. The following day, Beth had just gone out to the pool when I saw a girl of a similar age arrive which I took to be Manon, with her older sister, Chloé, and in tow Madame Audrey. I watched out of my bedroom window to see how Beth would take to each person as they walked up to the pool and set down their bags, and sure enough, Beth looked to be fine, and I thought to myself that maybe they were right. I chastised myself a little for being overly protective.

Beth had experienced bullying when she had attended her first school in Scotland. The unkind words and actions of the children had left scars and Beth, who was already hesitant prior to that about speaking to her peers, retreated further into her shell. It was for this reason that I protected her, but I also knew that she was going to have to figure this all out for herself at some point.

I continued to watch as they all spoke together and then, wanting to look like a friendly neighbour, pulled out some Magnum ice cream bars from the freezer and with a glass of iced water for each person balanced on a large tray, I went out to the pool to introduce myself. Madame Audrey was around my age, slim, dressed in shorts and a tee-shirt with short curly brown hair. Her face lit up as she saw me walking towards her as she stood there offering some sort of fruit that she had put into a bag and was sharing with everyone. I could see Beth tucking into some fruit as she sat with Manon by the pool and a feeling of relief came over me. I attempted to make some light conversation with Madame Audrey, which was based around weather and our beautiful garden, and feeling slightly awkward, I made my way back to my house where I planned to keep an eye on Beth from our terrace. Everyone seemed fine; Beth looked happy and relaxed. I chastised myself for making a fuss, a fuss in my own head, though, nothing spoken.

Marc had been working in the Alps now for three weeks. I was missing him because being married for eighteen years and being best friends, I had come to rely upon him, particularly for company as moving to France you cannot take any other friends with you. In my newfound situation where people were arriving in my garden without personally being invited, I needed someone to speak to, and whilst I could speak to Marc over the phone, it was clear he was living on a different planet to myself. Marc had in fact found himself working for a Scottish man, Ken, who weirdly enough came from the same town in Scotland that we had just left, which helped them to get off to a good start. Marc was sharing a large apartment in the middle of a small village with two other joiners who had come over from the UK. With Marc being within walking distance of a few restaurants and pubs, I could hear from his voice that he was relaxed and was fitting in well with the people surrounding him.

Marc was set up as an entrepreneur which meant that he was self-employed and paying his own tax and just had to put in an invoice every two weeks to Ken, who was project-managing the chalet renovations. This gave Marc the opportunity to look for his own renovation projects, although he had no intention of competing with Ken, who he now considered to be a good friend.

With steady money now coming in, Beth and I were able to visit restaurants, enjoy Friday-night pizzas and trips to the cinema, as well as stopping at our favourite *boulangerie* each week to load up on all our treats before spending the day at the beach.

Beth and I were overjoyed when Marc announced that he was to come home. It was only for a fleeting visit, he reminded us, but that was enough for Beth and I to start planning meals and what we were all going to do together. Beth and I realised early on after Marc had left that neither of us particularly liked what I cooked for our evening meals and that our menu was based upon what Marc liked as opposed to what we liked, plus Marc always insisted that we sat at the table to eat. We ditched the lot. With his announcement of his forthcoming arrival, we were back shopping for meat and veg and the table was cleared.

When Marc arrived home on Friday evening, to my surprise, he had the whole weekend planned. Saturday morning, we all got up and headed into Aix as Marc intended to buy a decent supply of chemicals for the pool as well as some warmer clothing he felt he might need when he expected the temperature to drop in the Alps. That morning, we left the house early around 9am, walked around Aix in the exhausting heat, stopped at the supermarket to pick up a few more supplies and were looking forward to coming back to the house, lunch on the terrace and spending the rest of the day lounging by the pool. Now that Beth could swim, Marc wanted to teach Beth how to dive.

A couple of weeks previously I had purchased some sun loungers, one for each of us, and I had them placed to the side of the pool. When we returned to the house and as the electric gates opened to allow us to drive into the garden, to our surprise we saw that there was a family sitting on our sun loungers having their lunch. On closer inspection, I could see that it was Madame Audrey, with a man I presumed to be her husband, along with her two daughters, Manon and Chloé. They waved over to us.

"Who are these people?" Marc asked, surprised and clearly annoyed.

"Antoine's cleaner and her family. It looks like they are making full use of being able to use the pool," I replied. As much as I liked Madame Audrey and her two girls, I was disappointed as it was the weekend, and I felt their presence was now encroaching on our family time. What was the best approach, I asked myself? If we were friendly, they would feel welcomed and able to come over when they wished, whereas if Marc showed he was not happy with their presence, maybe they would stop coming over. We decided the best option was to have our lunch on our terrace and stare them out.

Around 3pm, when they looked to have had their fun, they packed up and left and we spent the rest of the afternoon as we had originally intended in our pool having a diving competition. It had spoiled our day but as my sisters would often remind me when I had vented my woes, "Abi, this is another one of your first-world problems." It surely was, I agreed wholeheartedly, but it was still annoying!

As the weather heated up to nearly 40 degrees, we discovered that Antoine had a son who in turn had a girlfriend who in turn had a pesky dog. We knew this because they too made an appearance in the garden and spent numerous afternoons by the pool. It went along these lines…loud barking as the dog propelled itself out of Antoine's back gate, spotting Beth and chasing her crying back into our house, the continual shouting of their dog's name, their dog continuing to run off the lead with no thought to anyone else in the garden whatsoever.

I called to mind the conversation with Clément and his father when we took on the house: "Do not worry. Antoine, he has no friends, you will have the garden to yourself." Ha. Antoine's popularity was increasing daily as he set out to become the most popular man in Provence.

Chloé felt so at ease with venturing over to our garden that she was bringing her boyfriend and various other friends she was quickly picking up on the way. Antoine's son was now friends with Chloé and her friends, who together looked to be inviting everyone that they knew.

Beth confessed on many occasions that she was feeling uncomfortable with everyone coming around as she did not know who some of these people were. There were always new people arriving and Antoine never thought to ask if this was okay with either Beth or me. On one occasion as Beth was out swimming, Chloé and her new boyfriend were larking around splashing each other and he was lifting her up and throwing her down into the water. I had been watching Beth from the front terrace and saw that she had gotten out of the pool and was now lying on her sun lounger, so I continued to relax and read my book. As I did so, Beth had gotten up and opted to go back into the pool, and Chloé's boyfriend, looking to include Beth in their shenanigans, grabbed Beth from behind, lifting her high into the air and throwing her down into the water. I heard Beth's screams, and I dropped my book and ran over only to see my poor little girl under the water, gasping for breath. She had only just learnt to swim and here she was being tossed around. As Beth surfaced with water bubbling out of her nostrils and as she cleared her throat and spat out pool water, she was furious and started shouting and screaming at the boyfriend. Chloe and her boyfriend stared at me, not knowing what was going to happen next, but what was I going to say with such a small French vocabulary, so I chose to stare angrily at them. They stared back momentarily then proceeded to carry on as if nothing had happened. I wrapped Beth's beach towel around her and holding her close explained that they only wanted to include her in their fun, but it was falling on deaf ears, so I had no option but to manoeuvre my frightened and angry little girl towards our house.

Little by little, our days were being spoiled by other people. I had been hoping to catch Antoine to have a word, but he was now fully occupied with his new posse, and I could hear them all laughing and having a good time at the end of each day. It was difficult to get annoyed as he really did play the poor little lost boy rather well and there was a part of me that was happy to see him enjoying the company of others.

Clément had called in to see us on several occasions for a five-minute check, which seemed to be his allotted amount of time. Mia and I would laugh and say that he behaved like the rabbit in *Alice in Wonderland*, always in a rush to get somewhere.

"My brother, Abi, he is not correct, and the people that come to your garden, they are not correct. In France, we say of these people, *Tu donnes la main, ils prennent le bras.* Do you understand what I mean?" he asked me.

Yes, I understood fully what he meant, so I nodded in agreement. I was currently at my wits' end with it all.

"Maybe you want to speak with my parents, Abi, but I say now that they do nothing. Antoine, he take and take and they give and give. I have the family of sheet." He shook his head in despair and, concluding on that note, he got up from his seat by my garden table and left within his designated time.

I decided that a visit to Mia and Jean-Baptiste would be a good idea and so in the middle of August, when I could take the comings and goings in the garden no longer, I made my move.

As I approached their house, I noticed that all the shutters were closed, and I wondered if they were in, but I had heard no mention of them going on vacation, plus I doubted in this heat that either of them would have wanted to go anywhere, as it was hitting the 40s most days.

As I rang the doorbell, I peered into a very dark living space, not really expecting anyone to answer when Jean-Baptiste came out of the shadows and opened the door. Mia was shouting.

"This damn man of mine, he keeps closing all the shutters during the day to keep the heat out and I cannot do anything. I cannot stand this anymore." Mia seemed flustered and anxious, and I could see that I had picked a very bad time to speak about something that Clément had warned me may result in bad relations, both with them and with Antoine.

Not growing up in a hot country, I was unaware how irritable and annoyed people could become when one scorching day followed another, leaving everyone fighting for cool air and on the lookout for water to cool them down, either by drinking it or by jumping into it. Complaints about being unable to sleep, unable to breathe, etc., were subjects that I was quickly becoming used to. It was not affecting Beth and I too badly as we each had fans in our bedrooms and slept with just a sheet. With the bedrooms being upstairs, we kept the shutters closed during the day to keep the rooms cool and we seemed to be doing better than most, apart from our garden being taken over by what felt to be the entire neighborhood.

"Mia, I must speak with you about a situation in our garden that is giving Beth and I a lot of stress," I said as we sat across from each other at her dining table sipping from a glass of iced water.

"I think I know what you come to speak to me about, Abi. It is about Antoine and the people using the pool." Why would she not know? After all, I had spoken about it to Clément, and he would surely have warned her of my impending visit.

"When we came to rent the house, we were told that we would have full use of the pool and the garden if we were to maintain each. We purchase all the chemicals, clean the pool each day and maintain the garden and yet Antoine is inviting more and more people who neither clean the pool nor maintain the garden. They arrive, spend the day in the pool and leave. They have broken each of my three sun loungers and I never know at any point who is going to turn up." The words were pouring out of my mouth with the relief of finally being able to say how I felt in English.

Mia at this point asked Jean-Baptiste to join us at the table. Whilst he could not speak any English (supposedly), she wished him to be present as the property was in his name and not in hers. As he sat down beside her, she translated what I had just said to him. He looked over at me, clearly displeased at what I had said, and shook his head. He spoke to Mia and then Mia spoke to me.

"Abi, we understand your situation well. You are like me. You cannot always cope with people coming to see you uninvited. I am like that too." She was wearing a kind face but from what Clément had said to me, I was waiting for the excuses.

"My son is what I would class as special. He is a very demanding person and makes our life extremely difficult. Only this week he has come to me again to say that he has no money and that he has his credit card to pay and his tax. He has asked me for 10,000 euros. I am always giving him money. It pushes my relationship with Clément and my husband to the very limit. I do not know what to do with him. He is always complaining about how lonely he is and this year because of the pool he has many people coming to see him. You and I know well that they are using him. What exactly are you asking me to do as, being his mother, I want him to be happy because honestly, Abi, when he is happy it makes our life much easier," she explained.

I was taken aback yet again with information that to me should have been kept within the family. However, I realised that she and her husband (who was still shaking his head) were also at their wits' end with Antoine. I also realised that what I was about to ask was never going to happen, but I was here now, so I continued.

"Beth and I thought about a rota system that would allow us to share the pool. Do you think you could speak to Antoine, as we understand the weather is hot and his newfound friends want to use the pool, but we are paying for the use of the pool and they are not." I wanted to come across fair but also serious as this situation was affecting Beth and I, and we had enough stress to deal with at times.

She turned and translated this to Jean-Baptiste, who had changed his look from despair to anger. What I was asking, I could see, was only going to result in a massive family squabble, and by the look on Jean-Baptiste's face, he was making no effort to hide his dislike of his stepson.

"Abi, I go to ask Antoine, but I know exactly what he will say and I explain to you now that we can do nothing. The good news is that when September starts, there will be no one there as the French do not swim in September, it is too cold," she said, with her eyes begging me to drop the subject and leave.

Word had quickly gotten back to Antoine about my visit, as he marched over to see me on the same evening as my visit to his parents. I was sitting out on the terrace with Beth, running through some homework.

"Abi, what is wrong, why did you speak with my parents? You have a problem with my friends and family to use my pool?" he asked as he stood by my terrace, clearly angry. I noted the word *my* being stressed.

I reminded myself how awkward it would be in our first summer to fall out with this man. I had not fallen out with anyone since being a child at primary school and this situation brought back the uncomfortable situation I had with my best friend, falling out over something trivial. Antoine and I, prior to the influx of people, had been getting on well and I had invited him over to share a meal with us on several occasions. Never did I imagine that I would fall out with him, but considering how often the family fell out with each other, it did seem to be a matter of time.

"Antoine, I have no problem with your family and friends using the pool, but sometimes it is too much for Beth and I. I do not know who is in the garden and that is not a good situation when I have a young girl running around. I propose that we arrange a rota system," I replied, with as much strength as I could muster.

"No. I let you use *my* pool and if you want to use *my* pool then you must share it with other people," was his curt and angry response.

So, the pool was now his? The pool that had lain empty for the past umpteen years. The pool that no one was interested in until we turned up and asked to use it.

"That's fine," I said as I cut any further conversation dead and walked back into my house. The situation wasn't fine but what choice did I appear to have? It was the pool and garden of his parents and if they backtracked and said that he could invite all his friends over to use it, despite stating otherwise to us, then what could we do? We had a verbal not a written contract, so there was no proof of our agreement to show Antoine. We had no choice but to stay as it was apparent that we were not going to have the correct tax documentation to allow us to rent another house for at least another two years.

We decided to make the best of it. Suck it up maybe another expression.

Eight

Antoine

'*A man will never grow up if the people around him are always justifying his behavior*' was a statement I read when I opted to research why my neighbour was showing no indication of mentally entering adulthood despite being in his early fifties.

I am all up for weird and wacky people, there exists no personal rule of mine that necessitates that all my friends must share my opinions and ideologies, but there is a requirement that I put upon myself that I learn to understand the thought process of the people that I choose to have around me. It has never been a requirement that has previously put me under any great hardship and one that in truth I was most likely not consciously aware of until arriving in France.

Despite holidaying in this area of France on numerous occasions, it was becoming apparent that there existed a huge difference between holidaying in Provence and living amongst the people fulltime. As strangers came and went in our garden, dogs let off the leash unsupervised, dogs jumping into the pool and pooping on the terrace area we had set up by the pool and people blowing smoke in our faces, to Marc, Beth and myself, it all came across as disrespectful but to each of them it appeared to be normal. Were we at fault? Were we too British in our ways? Were we failing to adapt to French life? We decided that we should really try and accommodate as best as we could the holiday park that was now our garden and try to relax our standards.

As a family, we were enjoying living in Provence. The house and the garden and the pool all suited us, we had stopped worrying about money, Beth was settled at school, I was taking French lessons and continuing to work from home and each of us was taking full advantage of our blue-sky days. In truth, other than this unexpected influx of uninvited guests (uninvited by me, certainly), our life was pretty good. The fruit trees had burst into life, and we had a bountiful supply of figs, quince, cherries, plums, apricots, hazelnuts (or as Beth chose to call it, the 'Nutella tree') and pomegranates.

I was not just happy, I felt a deep inner contentment stemmed somewhat from having swapped a very competitive lifestyle for the reverse and here I was in my spare time pottering about a garden, picking fruit and making jam, and finding myself finally winding down from my previous fast-paced life. When we ate out, I rarely picked up on the conversations of others surrounding me. When I communicated, I said my piece and moved on. I was not in a rush to be fluent in French because I was enjoying being unable to tune in and the freedom that gave me. I liked being a foreigner, I could be who I wanted to be, or so I liked to believe.

The pool situation had taken me by surprise, but I did not want to blow the situation out of proportion as everyone else seemed to be having a good time and I continued to remind myself that I was living in their territory and that the onus was on me to adapt to their ways, not vice versa. As I lay in bed at night, I would consider how I could adapt better but I could not get into the mindset of those around me. I thought that I had, to some extent and to the extent that I wished to, but the more kindness that I had shown, the more I was being taken advantage of, as was the case with Antoine. What was going on with him and how could I resolve this situation without it blowing up again?

The answer came about one afternoon. It was early November, and I was in a pattern of visiting Mia not only to settle our monthly rent but also to sit and have a chat with her. We would cover every subject; religion, politics, books we had read and were currently reading, old movies, etc. We could talk together all afternoon and often this would be over a glass of wine or sometimes champagne if we were celebrating an event such as a birthday. This afternoon as we were chatting, Antoine appeared at the front door. Mia was not surprised and had mentioned to me earlier that he had spent the 10,000€ that she had finally given to him in August and here he was again asking for more money, this time 7,000€. She said that he had been asking her for this money now for several weeks and this time she was putting her foot down. If she gave in to him, she said, she would then have to offer the same amount to Clément because one way or another he would find out and that would lead to endless arguments with her husband.

I had noticed on each instance when I saw Antoine and Mia together that he would transform his face somehow into that of a pouting schoolboy. On this occasion, Antoine did not disappoint and with his sulky disposition he poured himself a drink and came to sit with us at the dining table. I hadn't spoken to him much since our last conversation relating to the proposed pool rota and, in truth, I was enjoying the break. He was the dark cloud that was threatening my blue sky.

Mia smiled at her son from across the table with what I could only describe as sad yet appreciative eyes before she announced,

"Abi, this is my little boy that I brought to Provence with me. He will always be my little boy. We came to Provence together when he was two years of age. He was my only companion until I met my husband. Antoine will always be that little boy to me."

And there it was – the creation of a monster!

Okay, fair enough, he wasn't exactly a monster but nonetheless her chosen method of upbringing was not helping matters, and from what I could grasp, she had allowed herself to be his bank account. She had explained that there were regular payouts each year and each year she resolved that there would be no more, but looking at his feeble expression, that he looked to have mastered several decades ago, he knew what strings to yank, and it was likely that he would get his way this time also.

A few days later and a very happy Antoine came walking around the corner towards my house with a smile from ear to ear. I knew Mia had relented, because Clément had told me, and I also knew that he went as far as threatening to take his own life. Wow…that was bad but seemingly it wasn't unusual. This was not someone that I wanted to be friends with, but equally it was not clever to fall out with him as it was becoming obvious that he could make matters worse for us because no one was out to challenge him. So that afternoon, having been given an insight into why he behaved the way he did, I made the decision to treat him in the way I would treat a child and not an adult.

Back to my family and during the holidays Beth had asked me if she could swap schools and go to the local French primary school, which was located in the next village. It was her idea and ultimately her choice. She had weighed up all the advantages, which went along the lines of:

- Longer lie-ins each morning
- Home for two-hour lunch break – she wasn't sure if she could, but she was going to ask
- Avoiding the long journey home at peak worktime traffic
- The ability to use her French that she had learnt
- To force herself to learn additional French

Whilst she had liked the international school, she did not feel that she was learning French fast enough. Marc and I were happy if she was happy and her list appealed to me too, so I made an appointment with the local school and signed her up. She was adept at making her own decisions and had previously back in Scotland asked me to swap her private school for the local primary, a decision that she never regretted. Only she knew what she could and could not cope with, after all, and reminded me very much of myself at that age.

With Beth settled at her new school, the pool drained and prepared for winter and the garden back to us, we waited to see what the weather would be like as we headed towards Christmas. Whilst the temperature in the early mornings and evenings had dropped, there were still many opportunities to go to the beach when days reached 17+ and most lunches we continued to take outside on the terrace. Evening meals were certainly taken inside with the open fire being stacked up and lit each evening, but the blue-sky days just kept coming.

When I reflected upon our first long hot summer, I found it amazing that when it chose to rain in Provence it would do so during the night, and each morning, with the sun high in the sky, everything would dry off within mini seconds. It was a weather pattern that I could most certainly live with. However, a week or so leading up to Christmas, we experienced a week of heavy rain which continued to come down all through the day and night.

One very dark and rainy afternoon as I was working at my desk in our living room, I heard someone running through the garden, because I could hear the splash of water as the person ran into puddles. Antoine arrived at my door dressed head to toe in denim, holding a rain jacket over his head, hair dripping and water running off his nose. What was the panic?

"Abi, I have run out of wine. Can I have some of yours and I will give you it back? I need for dinner tonight and tomorrow." His face was red with running and his usual cigarette was missing, possibly having fallen out of his mouth on his perilous journey across land to my house.

Antoine knew that I always kept a 10-litre box of table wine in the house that I would buy from my local *cave*, and I wasn't the best at telling lies, especially when the box was sitting on a shelf by the kitchen. I saw no option but to say yes and invited him in. He handed over a decent-sized bottle that he had brought with him but when I reached over to the box, I realised that I was running low, so I opted to fill half his bottle and return it to him.

"That is not enough. Do you think I could have more?" he asked cheekily as he failed to take the bottle from me. I could have said, 'Are you allowed to drink at your age, young boy?' and given him a telling-off, but I thought that would be taking the treating-him-as-a-child aspect too far, so instead I returned to the box and filled the bottle to the top. I was under no illusion that I would ever see a replacement coming from Antoine.

As we kept the conversation safe and discussed the weather, he informed me that his mother had told him to expect flooding over the next few days and as a precautionary measure for him to stack sandbags at his back kitchen door. Whilst it was raining heavily, I had not heard of any weather warning that the rain was to continue for any great length of time, and asked him if I too should do the same, as I did not want to get caught out, especially when Marc was away. He assured me that it was likely that his mother was panicking and that all would be fine and added that my house had never flooded but his had many years ago and Mia had never forgotten the devastation it had caused. He laughed at her worrying so and waved his hand as if to dismiss the silly notion that his house would flood again, and with that ran back out into the rain and back to his house, with my wine tucked under his arm.

Later that same afternoon, I had nipped out to buy more wine as well as some other shopping and to collect Beth from school. As I was running back and forth from my car to the house in the torrential rain, I failed to notice that I had left my driver door ajar.

That night, God decided to pour his vengeance on our small village and the heavens fully opened their gates. It was one almighty storm. It was compulsive viewing as I positioned myself by my bedroom window during the night, watching the garden flood and the lightning strike across the sky. Water covered our terrace, which concerned me, so I ran downstairs to check that it wasn't coming in the front door. Thankfully, the water stayed outside but I rolled up some towels and placed them to the back of the door just in case. I knew there was to be no good outcome and closed my shutters in the hope that I may be able to get some shut-eye.

A few hours later when morning arrived, I nervously opened my shutters. I was expecting more of the same, but the storm seemed to have turned things around and instead it was a beautiful sunny morning with a *Simpsons* sky. I was taken aback by the appearance of the sun, and it was difficult to imagine what we had just gone through, but the evidence was in the pool. The once emptied pool was now filled to the very brim and overflowing. I could not believe my eyes. I quickly got dressed and ventured outside.

By the look of the tide marks against the wall that surrounded my terrace, the water in the garden had reached just over half a metre during the night but had now subsided. I thought I'd better inspect my car and that is when I discovered that I had left my door partially open, and the water had poured in. Damn! I was thankful that it was an old car and went back into the house in order to get some containers to start bailing it out, as I had to take Beth to school, and without a pair of wellies it was going to be challenging.

It was still early at this point, around 7:30am, and once the car had been emptied, I left the doors open in the hope that the sun may dry it out prior to the school run. I was just about to make breakfast for Beth when Antoine came screaming around the corner of his house, tearing up to my house and shouting. I had seen him in various emotional states but this one topped the scale so far, as he looked like he had just been chased around the corner by a monster, or possibly the taxman.

"Abi, you must come to my house at once. It is a disaster." He was in a terrible state.

"Antoine, what is wrong? Is your house flooded?" I responded.

"Yes, you must come at once to help me. I have lost everything," he replied as he raised both hands up to his head in despair.

"It was quite a storm last night for sure," I said. "I thought my roof was going to come off, the noise was catastrophic."

"I never heard any noise last night," he replied rather sheepishly. "I think I drank too much wine."

Well, there went over a litre of wine in one sitting and now he was paying the price for being a drunken little schoolboy.

I explained that I was preparing breakfast for Beth and after that I would be taking her to school, and when my motherly duties had finished, I would call over to his house.

When I did make it to his house around 9am, wow, it was indeed a disaster. His back terrace was flooded and the water, instead of pouring over the side into a rain ditch, went directly into his kitchen and from there into his study, which was a significant area where he stored and repaired electronic equipment, in particular, computers. He had been exceptionally busy of late and had run out of counter space so had stacked the laptops on the floor. Everything that lay on the floor would therefore be ruined. That was bad enough and I hoped his insurance would allow him to reimburse his clients, but there was far worse to come because there was a basement area that was entered at the rear of the kitchen. This was his *cave*.

I had been down to Antoine's *cave* previously and whilst some French will use this to store their wine collection, in Antoine's case, he used it to store various other collections. I should mention that Antoine was an avid collector, and his *cave* contained the full collection of *Tintin* and *Asterix* comics and manuals, the *National Geographic* and various other magazines as well as some first-edition books, newspapers, playing cards, postcards, watch straps; the list could go on and on, which basically included anything that took his fancy and collections that he could persuade his mother to fund. His *cave* was full to bursting with everything that he had collected over the years.

Today, though, you could not see any evidence of his collections because the floodwaters had engulfed the whole of the basement and the water was up to the top of the stairs. Unless he had a separate collection of underwater diving gear that he kept in the storage facility next door, there was no hope of ever getting down into the *cave* to salvage anything. I doubted anything was salvageable other than the swords that I remember seeing; everything else would have to be thrown out.

"I must go to see the *mairie*," Antoine shouted as he stormed about with his head in his hands going from one room to the other, which was increasing his anger. "This is his fault for not fixing the rain ditch at the back of my house."

It was dawning on Antoine that he should have taken his mother's warning more seriously as it was the result of her house being flooded to the same extent that she had asked the *mairie* to put in a rain ditch to the back of their garden. This was the first opportunity with such a similar heavy downfall to see if the ditch had worked. It was clear that it hadn't.

"Abi, I give you a mop and a bucket for you to clean this for me," he ordered sharply as he passed over the mop and bucket and marched out of the house to go to see the *mairie*.

Did I have a choice? Didn't look like it, so I got on with the job of mopping and bucketing the water. An hour or so later, Madame Audrey's husband turned up and I could see by his sour expression that he too had been dragged into help. We both worked our socks off that morning and so much so that I got a phone call from the school, to ask had I forgotten to pick up Beth? What day was it? Ah, Wednesday, and she finished at 11:30. Shit! With all the activity, I had completely forgotten where I should be.

I turned up to school looking like I had spent several nights sleeping in the streets, picked up an embarrassed Beth and made it back home. I was exhausted, so taking a shower I got myself ready and came downstairs to relax.

"Abi." I could hear someone shouting my name again, and lo and behold, there was Antoine standing on my terrace, back no doubt to issue more orders.

"You haven't finished, there is still much work to be done," he said as he spoke to me like I was some naughty employee who was found slacking on the job.

I explained that Beth was now home from school and that I could not give him any more of my time until the following morning, and with that he shook his head angrily and wandered back to his house.

Stupidly, I returned the following morning, to face another barrel of orders. Madame Audrey's husband was also present with mop and bucket in hand and as I watched and listened to Antoine barking his instructions at us both, it reminded me of the children's story books of *Brer Rabbit,* who would always find ways to make others work on his behalf. Whatever we were doing, it was never going to be enough, so I walked off the job and left them to it.

After *Floodgate,* our second French Christmas was upon us. Marc was coming home for two weeks, and we had to think of a surprise present for Beth. We decided upon a metal detector.

The day after Christmas and we were out in the garden looking for treasure when Antoine came out to see what we were up to.

"I have a metal detector too," he said as he reached over to pick up Beth's new toy to examine it, before putting it down and announcing, "It is better than this one."

This was a grown ass man and he seemed to be competing with our ten-year-old. A week went by.

One morning as Marc was walking over to the *boulangerie* to buy breakfast, he spied Antoine in the garden with a metal detector. He chose to ignore him, picked up his croissants and came home, sneaking back into the house. We hoped Antoine would go away as this was our family time, and we were seldom altogether. He didn't go away and instead he started searching for treasure across from our terrace to make sure that we saw him. It was a matter of time before he came to see us. One, two, three… and there he was at the door.

"Do you like my new metal detector? It is the best one I could find. It is better than the one you bought for Beth." He stood there proud as punch. He really was competing!

It was apparent now that Beth's metal detector, which was chosen because it was within our affordable range rather than the best one ever created, had been better than the one he must have had, so apparently that set him on the search for a top-of-the-range model, which he was now showing off.

I recall shaking my head in disbelief and walking away, leaving him with Marc, and within a moment, Marc had dismissed him somehow and we all went back into the house and closed the door.

Turns out that Mia had paid for his new toy, and that this one was now part of a collection of three.

When Beth's birthday came around in July, we thought we would buy Beth a microscope. Again, it was within the affordable-but-fun range and when she wasn't using it, we asked her to place it on the sideboard by the front door to see what would eventuate. Beth was in on this game too.

Sure enough, when Antoine next came over, he spied the microscope. We waited a few days before Marc ventured over to see him, and there on his kitchen table was a new microscope, still in the box. If only I had a friend that owned a Ferrari that I could borrow for a few days.

Whatever we had, he wanted, whether it be tools that Marc had purchased, something for the house that I had purchased, or simply to copy whatever it was that we were doing. To a certain extent, we viewed it as unforeseen entertainment and opted to laugh, but he wasn't always entertaining enough to warrant a laugh.

The yellow jacket brigade had yet to form ranks to kick the ass of the then non-elected Emmanuel Macron, but no matter, there were enough angry people in France to get together to protest anyway and head on up to Paris to kick the shit out of the Champs-Élysées. What was this about? So far since relocating, I had watched this famous avenue being smashed up on both Labour days (1st May). It was a time for all the angry people, and there did appear to be a lot of these, to vent their frustration about whatever was getting them down. In truth, and I write more about this later in this book, my thought process is that it was a day to picture the Champs-Élysées as being your life, and with every kick you are imagining it being your partner, your parents taking too long to die to receive your inheritance, all the rich people you have ever known and read about and of course your employer, as Labour Day is bound to attract those that hate their employers. This may of course not be the thought process behind the continual protesting, but it was my guess.

Something was gearing up because Antoine was becoming angrier by the day as he scrolled and clicked his way through Facebook, which put him in touch with all the people who seemingly wanted to annihilate President Holland. Obviously, President Holland was responsible for everything. He was not a popular president but the longer I stayed in France, the more it appeared that the only popular and great presidents were those that were buried six foot underground.

Day after day, we listened to Antoine spurt out all his negativity about France. He insisted time and time again that Marc and I were never going to succeed living here as France had lost all their wealthy people and we would be lucky to ever buy a house or receive well-paid employment, etc. His chatter was truly exhausting, and it was getting us both down. Marc was doing exceedingly well, but we were not going to throw this into the ring as that was going to go down like a lead balloon.

I have never fitted in with the 'life's rugged highway' chatter, but when I have found myself in the company of this type of individual, I tend to just agree in order to keep the conversation flowing in a smooth fashion because disagreeing can end up in a dispute and is ultimately divisive. People think like they think and sometimes there is nothing that will ever change their thought process. Antoine's anger culminated one evening when he came stomping around the corner down the garden and over to our terrace. His face was red, his eyes were bulging, and he looked like he was going to explode. He was waving some piece of paper in his hands.

"That is it! I am taking my Kalashnikov and I go to Paris and I go to smash up the Champs-Élysées. I have had enough." He was angrier than I had ever seen him before, even angrier than *Floodgate*, so I knew that this was bad.

Marc and I glanced at each other and then to Antoine and back again to each other. There was an irate boy standing on our terrace who claimed to have a Kalashnikov. What should we do with him?

"Antoine, come on, calm down. Come have a beer with us." Marc was a laid-back dude and thought beer was the remedy for everything.

The outburst had been caused by the arrival of a letter from URSSAF. If you have never heard of this French tax department, think yourself lucky, as whilst I have no way of proving my theory, this is a dedicated and elite team that have been trained directly by members of the Gestapo. They show no mercy, and it is not unusual to have a letter arriving on your doorstep indicating that you owe them a considerable amount of money that you had no idea you had to pay. Marc and I were expecting such a letter as everyone we knew since arriving in France had received one, and here on our terrace was a very angry Frenchman who had received one of URSSAF's famous demands and this one was for 36,000€. A figure that they were insisting was to be paid in one go. It was fair to say that he was lucky if he had 36€ in his bank account, and it was also fair to say that he had reason to be angry and maybe even fair to say that the use of the Kalashnikov may have been a good idea.

After a few beers and outstaying his welcome by several hours (which was his way to ensure that he stayed for dinner), he seemed to calm down, and we learnt that he had in fact being paying his tax, so we convinced him that it must be a mistake on the part of URSSAF and his accountant should be able to sort it all out.

A few weeks passed by and when Marc had returned home and had ventured over to have a few beers with Antoine, he was informed that it was indeed an error on the part of URSSAF and they had reduced the amount to 13,000€. He did not have 13,000€ but his mother did, so it was just a case of asking her for it and he seemed happy enough with this idea as he sipped his beer.

I dreaded my next visit to see his parents.

Winter had passed quickly, lots of sunshine, the odd weekend at the beach and a few days up with Marc; the house was warm enough and very little happened other than the usual daily routine.

Our second summer had finally arrived and knowing the events of the previous year, we knew that we were likely to have May and June to ourselves, the necessity to share the pool with half the village in July and August, with September returning to us again. At least we knew this time and could devise a plan. We had planned to use the pool when we could in July and go up to see Marc in August or take a holiday over to Italy, whatever Marc could squeeze in, allowing for his busy summer work schedule.

It was mid-July, and the usual suspects were starting to come out of the woodwork and a few new faces as well, as was to be expected. Beth and I were opting to swim later in the evenings, and one such evening as we were racing up and down on our favoured inflatables, I spied someone coming out of Antoine's back gate. It must have been around 11:30pm. We only had the pool lights on, which did not light up any other part of the garden as we did not want to draw attention to ourselves, although with all the noise coming from the pool it was likely that sound travelled further than we realised. I initially got a scare but as the person approached into the light, I could see that it was Antoine, and my frightened state intensified.

Standing before me was my neighbour, who up until this evening I had rarely ever seen in a pair of shorts, but here he was dressed only in a very revealing pair of Speedos. (Is there any other type?) Gold medallion was absent; mass of chest hairs remained. In one hand, he had a bottle of gin and in the other, two glasses containing ice, lemon and tonic.

Beth had stopped playing by now and stood, like me, riveted to the spot. She looked over at me and I at her as we widened our eyes with the same look of…what the…?

"I go to the supermarket. I know you like gin and tonic," he said, "so I bought some for you. I thought we could drink it together tonight." He was regarding me with what I can only describe as a look of desire. Had I missed something? A bar mitzvah maybe? What a time to choose to grow up.

What could I say? Another deep breath.

"*Wow, c'est superbe ! J'adore le gin et tonique.*" That is not what I wanted to say, but that is what came out of my mouth.

Were Beth and I to have no time on our own? I was thinking. Poor Beth, she was at her wits' end with this boy.

Antoine placed the bottle and the glasses down beside me and I stood aside as he prepared to dive into the water. It was a good dive too, not quite Pierce Brosnan in *Mrs Doubtfire*, but impressive nonetheless. He swam up to the deep end and back down to me, and as he stood up at the shallow end, he ran both his hands through his hair and stood there smiling up into my eyes.

He poured the gin into each glass and leaned in beside me. "*Notre santé*, Abi," he said as he continued to gaze into my eyes. "*Notre santé*, Antoine," I replied quickly, looking away. What was this? A friendly neighbour? A horny neighbour? I could not tell but he was French, and my encounters with Frenchmen up until this point told me to be careful, so I played safe and went with horny. I asked him what music he enjoyed listening to and loaded up some tunes to listen to so we could focus on music as a subject. It was the least enjoyable gin I have ever drunk, in the most uncomfortable setting, and it was becoming clear the closer he got to me that I had to find an escape route. Looking over at Beth, I announced how tired she looked and that it was long past her bedtime. With that, she yawned as she too saw her chance to escape and we hopped out of the pool, thanking Antoine for a lovely evening as we sauntered back home. It was a difficult walk as, in truth, Beth and I wanted to run for our lives.

Beth was spitting chips as, like me, she enjoyed doing her own thing and was fine with visitors if they were invited or just passing through, but Antoine was a demander of time, my time, which when she was home was supposed to be her time. Her mind, unbeknown to me, was formulating a plan.

Antoine had a habit of parking his car outside our kitchen window, which was directly below our bathroom window. He could have parked outside his own house but why would he do that when he could park it outside ours? The bathroom window was often open, and Marc and I had both noticed that there was something scattered on the roof of Antoine's car, and sometimes it was also spread out over the front windscreen and bonnet. What on earth was it? Clément too had commented on the mess of Antoine's car as he stopped to have a beer with us and would say:

"Why my brother not clean the car? He does nothing."

Antoine, however, never seemed to notice, and he certainly did not speak to us about it. Instead, he just got into his car and drove off with whatever was on his roof sliding about and tipping down onto his windscreen. This had been going on for several weeks.

One day as Marc and I were sitting on the terrace, we heard a noise coming from the bathroom window, with something clearly being poured out of the window. We realised that it could only be Beth, so I ran upstairs to see what she was up to. I found her at the window with a glass in her hand.

"What are you doing, Beth? Are you pouring something out of the window?" I asked, as I could clearly see that I had caught her in suspicious circumstances.

"Mum, I am just pouring some water out of the window," she replied, doing her utmost to look innocent.

I looked out of the window and sure enough there was water on the roof of Antoine's car. As I looked down onto the floor by the bathroom window, however, I could see what looked to be scatterings of washing powder and then it dawned on me.

"Have you been emptying washing powder onto Antoine's roof by any chance?" I asked.

She had the guiltiest face I had ever seen. "Mum, I do not like Antoine. He is at our house all of the time and I want him to go away. I just wanted to do something bad to him because I am so fed up with him being here. I have put washing powder on his car for a long time now and I wanted him to be angry, but he has never said anything, and I am angry at that."

I stopped to think. This situation with Antoine coming over had caused our little girl to take matters into her own hands. Could we blame her?

Marc suggested I go over to see Antoine with some excuse to take up his time, to allow Marc the chance to wash down his car. To our relief, there was no lasting damage and on the plus side, Antoine's car was the cleanest we had ever seen it, although we doubted he would notice.

Neither of us could blame Beth for her actions. I found myself that night doing what I do best and laughing. My laugh a combination of stress, nervousness and the sheer ridiculousness of our situation. I seemed to be laughing all day every day since I had arrived in France.

Before I finish this chapter, I should mention that Antoine turned up at my door several weeks after *Floodgate* with a potted orchid and thanked me for helping him. It was highly likely that his mother told him to buy it for me, told him to thank me and gave him the money but, unusually, on this occasion I received no confirmation through the grapevine.

I should also mention that his mother dug her hands into her deep pockets once again and paid off his tax bill.

Nine

...they take the whole arm

In year three, thanks to Marc's incredible determination and hard work, we had what we could class as a 'lifestyle'. Work at the ski resort was booming and it seemed endless, everyone looking for the perfect chalet with the perfect view and a perfect interior. Marc was in his element. In truth, we should all have been together living in the Alps, but with Beth having started *college** and with all of us enjoying our time in Provence, we each seemed happy enough to keep things the way they were. It also meant that when Marc came home in the summer, we did not have to rely upon staying at home and were finally able to go on holiday.

The family continued to inform us on a regular basis that France was on a downward spiral and that Marc was never going to earn much money. The government, they assured us, was useless

---

* The equivalent of secondary school in the UK

and there was no money to be earned. As the money gathered pace, I was bursting with positivity. However, being surrounded by such negativity and a doom-and-gloom mentality, I felt that I had no one to share my enthusiasm with. When I spoke to each family member, I got the distinct feeling that they were expecting me to turn up one day to announce that we had ran out of money, couldn't pay our rent and were heading back to the UK, when it could not be further from the truth.

Mia and Jean-Baptiste were certainly not in the same category of doom as Antoine; however, they did seem to absorb the questionable 'facts' coming out of his mouth. On one occasion, they enlightened me that the Chinese were buying up all the farms in France and were going to take over. Antoine had a good source, they said. I knew his source and laughed.

I wondered sometimes if they wanted us to fail, or was it more of an expectation? We had come to France knowing just enough French to get us by. We had arrived with no means to purchase a house and no paperwork to rent one. Whilst I was working from home earning a meagre income, Marc had arrived with no work. Adding all of this up, I suppose we made no sense whatsoever to a family who lived and breathed money and seldom left their own village. We were poor in their eyes, and I think the word *crazy* could well be used to describe maybe how they saw us as a family, but on our side of things we were also happier than we had ever been.

In an attempt to show them that we were not crazy, and did in fact have a plan, we presented the before and after house schedules of the homes that we had renovated in the UK, with one appearing in a home/design magazine. We were trying to put across, that we had enjoyed a good lifestyle but had gambled on the housing market for too long and had finally lost. They nodded to understand what had happened then questioned why we had opted at that stage to come to a poor part of Provence. This family understood money, but we could see from how they lived that they did not understand the competitive nature of what Britain had become and the yearning we had to find ourselves a simpler way of life.

We had come to terms, somewhat, with what to expect in the summer months and knew that if things got overbearing, we could escape up to the Alps to stay with Marc, who was now living on his own in a two-bedroom village house. It felt good to have options.

As we crept into August, temperatures soared to over 40 degrees. One morning, after trying and failing to sleep in my sauna that I had fond memories of once existing as a bedroom, I got up to open the shutters. It must have been around 9:30am. I was tired, exhausted, overheated and extremely grumpy.

Upon opening one of my shutters, I looked over to the pool and to my surprise I saw Jean-Baptiste swimming. Where was Mia? Just then, I stuck my head out a little further and to my dismay I saw her sitting in her wheelchair, with Antoine behind it, and they looked to be ambling over to my terrace. What?? I had no gate or fence around my terrace, so it had become a bit of a free-for-all. It was partially my fault as I could see that the weather was heating up and had mentioned to them to come over to use the pool. It was their pool after all. I enjoyed their company, I found them to be good people and supportive to my situation, taking me to the garage, for example, if my car had broken down, letting me take on a little room attached to another part of the outside house so that I could have a third bedroom. I had already invited them over on several occasions to have lunch with Marc, Beth and I, and we even threw an engagement party meal by the pool when they had some visitors arriving from the States. Opting to use the pool in the morning made perfect sense as by the afternoon at 40+ it was way too hot, plus way too busy, or a better word would be *congested*.

Mia and Antoine were chatting as they headed towards my house and I hoped that they had not spied me hanging out of the window, so I quietly and slowly closed my shutter and jumped back into bed to think of a plan. I couldn't go downstairs now to make coffee as my coffee machine made too much noise grinding, and they would certainly hear it as they were only a couple of metres away. I lay on my bed and after a few moments I could hear Antoine shouting my name. I chose to play deaf. There was only one door out of my house and so I decided to stay in my bed and wait it out. I should also mention that I never step foot out of my door until I have my make-up on, and my hair done...it only takes me around twenty minutes as it is not a layered approach, but during those precious minutes a miracle occurs. Inviting them in for coffee with my out-of-bed face was surely going to result in a discussion on their daily family hotline. This was a family who were each born with a set of eagle eyes. Nothing escaped their attention, and with Clément driving back and fore past my house and Antoine coming over on a regular basis, everything was reported back to Mia. I had no plans to give them anything more to gossip about, as gossip they would!

Go away, go away, go away, I kept saying to myself until finally, around twenty minutes later, when my name had stopped being called, I heard them leave. I should mention that a small ramp had been installed from the garden up into my terrace and I had chosen not to remove it as it allowed Mia to come over to see me when she called in to see Antoine. Removing it would have appeared rude. I breathed a sigh of relief and went down to make coffee.

Once presentable, I wandered out to the garden and feigned that I had a rough night's sleep and had only just gotten up.

"You must have slept well, as I was waiting for you this morning. Did you not hear me?" Mia asked, looking a little put out. She could be very direct at times, which often took me by surprise, especially as I was a tenant, not a member of the family.

"I am so sorry. No, I never heard a thing," I lied. "The weather is stinking hot, and it is very difficult to sleep."

Later the same day, Antoine announced to me that he had some friends coming down from Paris to stay with him, something about a girl he used to know who had recently contacted him through Facebook. In the same conversation, he announced that his stepsister and her husband and two children were coming to stay the last two weeks of August. I had met them briefly the previous year and they were delightful and very respectful too concerning our privacy. They got the picture, unlike everyone else. With the continual stream of new visitors, it was certain that he was either sitting on his roof each evening with a top-of-the-range talking drum from West Africa or else had joined a Facebook page for people who wanted a freebie holiday.

With the whole Franglais chat that existed between us all, I hadn't picked him up as to the date his friend was arriving, although I knew it was to be in August. One early afternoon, just after lunch, I was sitting working at my desk with a stack of work to get through and I heard a car at the gates tooting its horn. Who was this? I opted to ignore it and carried on working but they beeped the car horn again, so I went out to see who it could be.

It was a man and woman, maybe early to mid-forties with a little girl around three strapped into the back seat of their estate car, and in the very back, an enormous hairy dog was huffing and puffing. They fitted the brief description of the family Antoine had mentioned, apart from the hairy dog, so I went back into the house to collect the fob to open the gates to allow them to enter the garden. Who had given them permission to park in the garden? A brief chat to allow me to point them in the direction of Antoine's house and I went back to work.

The family were up first thing in the morning and had positioned themselves on my new replacement sun loungers, looking to make a day of it by the pool. Their hairy dog was bounding up and down the garden, in and out of my terrace. It was like something out of a comedy sketch, but this morning my humour had packed up and left town. A morning swim, we could see, was now out of the question for this week as opting to take a swim meant chatting, which meant Beth being excluded again, and the French love to talk…they can talk for hours! I may come across as rude to you, but my patience was wearing thin and whilst I did make the effort to speak to this lady, and she was delightful, it was now of no significance to me if these people were nice or not. They were just all after a freebie holiday in the South of France with someone they had looked up from the dark distant past. This lady mentioned that she had met Antoine over a decade ago when a mutual friend set them up on a date. It wasn't a relationship that she wished to pursue and instead stayed in touch with Antoine as a 'friend'. Looking at how grumpy her husband was with her and their little girl, I thought that maybe she would have done better to have kept him too as a 'friend' because the way in which he spoke to them was making Beth and I livid. Even Antoine made an appearance on our terrace one evening to vent his concern about the way in which this husband was choosing to speak to his family. It was making their stay very awkward, Antoine had added, and did I want to come over to join them one evening for a meal and drinks to see if that would make things easier? How many languages could I think of to say no in?

She was a very nervous lady and had brought with her a dog that she had trained to protect her. Sure enough, wherever she went in the garden this big hairy hound would bound over to be with her. A very odd family.

Beth and I had a confab. We now had a grumpy misogynistic father in our garden, Antoine's Parisian family were due to arrive, and the usual suspects and friends were visiting daily. Stepping outdoors was like entering an oven. We made the decision that it was time to jump in the car and head for the hills.

There was a problem, though, as I had a garden full of pot plants, a mixture of flowers and herbs that I had grown from seed.

They were my little babies but who was going to care for them when I was not around? Antoine had mentioned to me that when I was planning to go to the Alps to tell him, as in that way, he would keep an eye on my house. Antoine thinking about anyone other than himself? I had grave doubts, but anyway, I would trial him out.

I thought that the best way to ensure that my plants would be watered was to place them in the main garden where an underground water sprinkler system was automatically set to come on twice a day during the summer months. I waited until the system was working and chose my spot carefully. I called around to see Antoine and explained what I was doing with my plants and how precious these were to me. I brought him out to the garden to show him where I had placed all the pots and he assured me that he would keep an eye on them.

"Do not worry, these will all be fine, Abi. Go and have a good holiday," I recall being his parting words.

With the much-needed reassurance, Beth and I happily packed up and headed up to the coolness of the mountains.

Marc's place was in a very small mountain village. It was a mid-terraced mountain house over two floors. Two bedrooms and a bathroom on the ground floor and an open-plan kitchen, dining and living area on the first floor. It was a good space for us all, plus where it was situated, it did not get direct sunlight, so it was refreshingly cool. Marc was still using a winter quilt, whereas in Provence we were each sweltering under a light cotton sheet. Snuggling down under a quilt was joyful.

Beth and I had a wonderful three-week break; cycling, visiting refuges (mountain houses that become restaurants in the summer months), swimming in the lakes and picnicking. As we arrived towards the end of our three weeks, we were happy to be going back to Provence. By this point, our blood had cooled down and we were missing the heat!

As Beth and I arrived back at our house, the first thing I did was to check my plants. To my absolute horror, every single plant was dead. They looked to have been fried alive, so ultimately a cruel death for the plants that I worked so hard to nurse into life. What made the situation more brutal was knowing that Antoine would have been out by the pool with his family each day or at least having a few beers by the pool and would have to have walked by my plants.

On the plus side, the garden was joyfully quiet, and the temperature had dropped back to something more bearable. When I did see Antoine again, I made no mention of the plants and neither did he. There was a vindictive side to this boy that made its appearance now and again, and I gathered that my plants dying gave him pleasure, of some sort or other. At least someone may have gotten something out of it.

That year, Beth and I chose to spend Christmas with Marc in the Alps. Marc was now good friends with Ken, the man whose advert Marc had responded to on Gumtree, and unbeknown to Beth and I, Ken had a surprise lined up for us all. Christmas that year was to be enjoyed in a two-star Michelin restaurant.

The restaurant that Ken had selected was perched on the top of Europe's highest ski resort and the views were unbelievable. Upon entering, we could see that it was a very relaxed atmosphere with some guests still in their ski gear awaiting their Christmas lunch. Servers were wearing sweatshirts and had a respectful yet casual approach as we were shown to our large table, seating all 9 of us. Ken had insisted that we each try the ten-course tasting menu which he and his wife had enjoyed on a previous occasion, so despite the cost set at 250€ per person, we went ahead with his advice and over the course of that outstanding afternoon, we were served plate upon plate of the most incredible food.

We had high hopes and, as is common with French cuisine, it exceeded our expectations. It was an afternoon to cherish, as it was only a short period of time after this day that Ken was diagnosed with life changing health issues that led him and his family to pack up and move back to Scotland.

It was not the best start to the year as my Alfa had broken down now on two occasions. On one occasion, I had to get a taxi home and had no cash on me so had to run around to Antoine's to borrow some. Fortunately, he had his family from Paris staying and collectively they lent me the money to pay the driver and to my surprise they suggested that Antoine towed my car back to the house. I adored his Parisian family. They were very kind and obliging people. Antoine shocked me further by suggesting that I use his car when mine was in the garage, which I took him up on for the two necessary days. We seemed to be getting on better, to the point that when his birthday came around, I baked him a chocolate birthday cake. Children love birthday cakes, and he was no exception.

My old Alfa, I could sense, was coming to the end of its life. Beth and I were up and down now to the Alps regularly as well as back and forth to the beach, plus taking the occasional day trip to explore other cities and villages. It was time for a change. We had a bigger budget this time around, thankfully, and Marc spotted a car that he knew I would fall in love with. It was a black Audi A3 with black leather interior. For me, this was like trading up to a Ferrari. I had forgotten what it was like to have Bluetooth and air conditioning. Fortunately, the car was still available and when I saw it, it was love at first sight. When the dealer approached Marc, Marc explained that we had an Alfa to trade in. In my head, they were going to look at my car and offer me 2€, but to our surprise and delight they asked Marc what he was hoping for a trade-in. Marc spluttered, "2,000 euros?" I nearly choked. The dealer didn't appear to laugh and instead had a good look around. "How about 1,000 euros?" It was 998€ more than I had expected so the deal was done.

I loved going back to basics, but I would be telling humungous porkers if I said that I had not missed having a nice car. To my credit, I felt that I had carried off my Alfa very well as I know that I had shocked my family when I had traded down and was driving what they may have described as a 'banger'. There was a part of me that day when I collected my car that wanted to gaze upon it all day and all night, such was my overwhelming feeling of happiness. I could not have been any happier if it was a Ferrari. To my new adopted family, however, it may well have been such a car; such was their response to something that was ultimately none of their business.

Marc was home and he was out giving the car a wash and a polish one sunny morning when Antoine came stomping around the corner.

"Why did you buy Abi this car?" he demanded. "She could have used mine. She did not need another car." He appeared to be angry with Marc.

Marc was taken aback by his abrupt and enraged outburst. "It was time for Abi to change her car and she adores the Audi, so I wanted her to have something that she loved," Marc chose to respond.

I wasn't present and Marc, being a dude, isn't always great at recalling who said what, so I do not know what happened next other than Antoine seemed to be put out and stomped back home in the manner that he had arrived, clearly unhappy with our new set of wheels.

When I was next up to see Mia to pay the rent, I casually mentioned that Marc and I had bought another car, but I could see by the frown she was wearing that she already knew. She looked to be extremely displeased with me and as she sat on the edge of her bed listening to my excited chatter, she continued to direct her attention to the floor, shaking her head occasionally and finally lifting her head and changing the subject as she was prone to do, starting with the words, "Well..."

What was going on? I was getting the distinct impression that they were not happy with our decision to buy this car. They could not be jealous, because they themselves had a luxury German car parked in their driveway, far more expensive than ours, and we were renting one of their houses. Could it be that they wanted us to fail? Or was it because they continually told us that we could not succeed in France, and here we were proving them wrong?

A month later, once things had settled down and our new car was finally old news, Marc was home for a long weekend and Antoine came over to have a beer with us as we sat under the tree in the sunshine. We each talked over our plans for the year. Antoine mentioned that his son would be turning thirty early May and that he would like to throw a party for him. I love the idea of parties but have seldom been to a good one, so the thought of creating one rocked my boat.

A real party. It was going to mean a garden full of people, but that was nothing new as I had gotten to know half of Provence already by this stage and thought that we might as well just rustle up a few strays that had missed Antoine's invite.

Antoine's son, Thomas, had plumped for a Hawaiian-themed party. This seemed to go down well with everyone, especially Beth, who had begged me to take her to the party shop to give her the chance to select her costume. The Hawaiian theme seemed to be a popular choice as half the shop was dedicated to it. Once at the shop, Beth selected her *lei* and a pair of floral plastic sunglasses, which she chose to wear every day leading up to the event.

Antoine had opted to organise the main course, which he referred to as a *big plate,* a meal he described as a selection of different meats gently cooked over a slow heat using a large paella pan sitting on a gas stove. Once the meat was cooked, rice was added, and this resulted in a large plate of food that everyone could queue up to help themselves to. We recalled him speaking about the *big plate* on many occasions as it had been served at a family get-together he had attended several weeks back and to be fair, he hadn't stopped talking about it ever since. Each time he mentioned the *big plate* he would raise his index finger and his thumb together up to his mouth and kiss them, indicating that this was one tasty dish. He sold it well and it seemed a practical way to feed everyone.

I had hosted a few family dinners and lunches by now for Antoine's family and I knew that other than Mia and Jean-Baptiste, everyone else turned up empty-handed. Bringing a bottle or two of wine did not seem to be customary in this part of France, and therefore I had to think ahead to the party as I expected people to bring nothing other than themselves.

To Do Lists. I doubted Antoine had ever clapped eyes on one, but this was about to change as I had the distinct impression that he was leaving everything to me. I typed up a list in French and took it over to him. I could see by his face as he read through it that he was not expecting to do anything...and that face told me that I had indeed made the right decision.

The list (more or less):

- Buy enough wine for everyone
- Find jugs to pour the wine into (I saw heaps of jugs in the store next door)
- Gather up cutlery from everyone you know
- Sort out plates and glasses – I had mentioned that paper plates and paper cups were for the parties of children, so if he could, try to round up real plates, but plastic wine glasses were an option and paper napkins were fine

That was it. Simple really and I would organise the rest.

Mia and Jean-Baptiste had come up with the idea of renting tables and chairs from the local *mairie* as in that way the *mairie* was also being notified of the evening of the party in case there were any complaints. It was the first time that I had been made aware of the necessity to inform the *mairie* of a forthcoming party, but it made sense.

Party day came upon us. We knew because at around 9am we heard something going on outside on our terrace and to our surprise, there was Thomas setting up some picnic tables with his sound system and computer and was starting to play his music… loud. Had he asked us to use our terrace? Nope. Like father, like son. We let it go…it was party day after all and this was the birthday boy.

With decorations hanging from every tree, coloured paper table covers, an inflatable palm tree cooler, which was to be filled with beer, and a Hawaiian-skirted table that I had set up under a tree with a flowery sign stating *SERVEZ-VOUS PUB,* it was all coming together nicely.

The tables were not very wide, and we had opted to have them in one long line, so I was looking for an entrée that would include the table decorations. To do this, I bought ten pineapples, removed some of the inner leaves and placed in the inside of each a yellow candle. I went with the good old '70s cocktail sticks with pickled onions, saucisson and cheese cubes, which were to be pierced into each pineapple. Baskets of bread as well as tubs of dips on each table to ensure there were some options. Beth and Marc were busy preparing the starters in the kitchen as I ran about with my *to-do* list ensuring that everything else was in order.

It was around 7pm and guests were starting to arrive. Music was playing, the theme was set, but still no cutlery, wine jugs or wine. It was time to go find Antoine.

He had forgotten about the cutlery and the wine jugs but had remembered about the wine and had bought 2 x 5 litre boxes: one red and one rosé.

"Antoine, that is never enough wine," I said. "I only have enough for one third of the table if I pour each into jugs."

"Oh, it is nothing," he replied. "I have lots of other alcohol on the bar table."

It was true he had bought some bottles of spirits and some soft drinks, but this was France, surely everyone would want to have wine flowing throughout the meal. Antoine could see my agitation so assured me.

"They are French. If they want wine, they can ask for it. Do not worry, Abi, it will be fine." And with that off he went to find the jugs.

And if they ask for more wine, I thought, do you have any? I knew the answer to that.

There was also another matter concerning the *big plate* that was being cooked up by Simon, an uncle of the family. I had watched him set up to the side of the pool around 10am that morning and I had also watched him opening bottle after bottle of beer. The smell coming from the plate was wafting over to my house and it did smell good, but as I watched this man, I was wondering if he was going to be able to remain sober enough to serve what he was cooking.

I dug out all my cutlery, sent Jean-Baptiste home to collect what he could find, and combined now with Antoine's, we had enough. Antoine had finally collected all the jugs and I started to empty the boxed wine into each. I was right...one third of the way up the table and I had run out of wine. I had a 10litre box of red wine in my house, but I wasn't for sharing this past my own table, so two jugs were filled for our end that at least allowed me to spread the jugs out so that the top table at least had some.

We were all set.

Around 8:30pm it began to rain. Fortunately, in amongst Antoine's many collections in the store house he seemed to have rolls of polythene and quickly the tables were covered up. The rain stopped after around fifteen to twenty minutes and a breeze took its place, which blew out all the candles. It was the first evening that it had rained in weeks…typical! When things start to go wrong, I remind myself that booze normally helps, so with that in mind I returned to my house and poured myself a large G&T.

Thomas had created a playlist that appealed to all ages as I watched children dancing and singing and the older guests tapping their feet as the disco lights flashed in unison. The party had well and truly kicked off. I was distributing canapés and chatting to the guests, ensuring that they each had a drink in their hand. Time was ticking away; it was now 9:30pm. It wasn't quite so warm anymore and I could see the oldies rugging up, so I mentioned to Thomas if we could prepare everyone to sit down to start our meal.

"No, I must wait for some friends to join us as they do not finish work until 10pm." His reply was somewhat sharp, and I could see that he was oblivious to many of his guests huddling in groups questioning if we were ever in fact going to eat.

Time for an intervention. I had a word with Jean-Baptiste and Mia, who agreed that enough was enough and they gave me their agreement for me to do what I was about to do.

I went over to my terrace, moved Thomas' laptop to one side, turned down the music, climbed on top of the table, clapped my hands and shouted for everyone's attention. In my best French, I announced that it was finally time to sit down to eat. I gave them our apologies for the delay as we were waiting for some late guests to arrive. To my surprise, I was met with a sea of blank faces; my best French was not cutting it. Thankfully, one of the children present, maybe eight years of age, came running up knowing exactly what I was trying to convey, and climbing up beside me, she spoke to everyone in their own lingo. Everyone laughed and went "Aah" (that's what she meant) and proceeded to take their seats.

Mia and Jean-Baptiste, along with his sister, sat down at our end, along with Marc and Beth. Beth had been running about earlier in the evening with some of the children who had arrived and appeared to be having a good time, but she too was starving and very frustrated with goings-on, so she ended up in the kitchen making herself sandwiches. This was not a concern, but strangers entering my house asking to use the toilet was, and I had asked Marc to go in to look after Beth as I went to find Antoine to ensure that he spoke to everyone and directed them to use the toilet in his house and not ours.

I was happy to finally sit down with everyone to start our meal but within around five minutes of doing so, I had different people, one by one, coming down to ask me where the wine was.

"See that man over there?" I said in French as I pointed over to Antoine. "That is the person you need to ask, not me." It was clear that our visitors had arrived empty-handed other than to bring some birthday gifts. I had previously read, in a French magazine that I had purchased on French etiquette at the local supermarket, that gifting wine can be seen as an insult if the host has taken the time to select fine wines for the food he or she plans to serve. I understand that perfectly. However, in our case, we were living in small-town France, '70s starters, one big plate of something or other and a birthday cake. There was no requirement for Parisian etiquette as this was not a scenario that required fine wines, and gifting the host with several bottles of wine would have gone down well and saved the evening. Our host had given zero thought to what was to be served even though we were surrounded by field upon field of vines and had a plentiful supply of good quality and inexpensive boxed table wines on our doorstep, and yet he had opted to buy the cheapest boxed wine from our local supermarket!

I had left some wine in each box and had set them on the bar, and I saw Antoine pointing over in that direction, upon which the two men grabbed a box each and walked back to their seats. Good luck, I thought, as there was barely two glasses' worth left in either of them. I noticed that one of the men who had lifted the boxed wine was the cook. I had a bad feeling.

Entrée completed, and Antoine stood up to announce that he had arranged for a *big plate* for the main course and if they each could take their plates up to the chef to be served. As I sat with Mia discussing world events, Antoine came running down to our table in a panic.

"Abi, there is a mistake. Simon, he has not put in the rice. It is just meat and liquid." Antoine was furious as he looked down at his plate of bones. "He had one job, he had all day. Why did he not say that he had forgot to buy rice?" Antoine came across this time as someone who had actually spent his own money. He was just about in tears.

"Antoine, it is too late now, do not worry. There is plenty of bread and people can use that for the gravy," I assured him. "Go, get drunk and forget about it. There is nothing you can do now."

I had topped up our jug of wine now on two occasions despite begging looks from our adjacent table. Serves you right for not bringing any, was my thought process. There were just over seventy people sitting around this large table that stretched from the end of my terrace up to the tall trees at the back of the garden. The lights of the swimming pool were on, as were all the Hawaiian lights we had hanging from the trees, creating a wonderful ambiance that matched the chilled-out music selected by Thomas.

Beth was next to come scurrying down to see me, shoving her plate full of bones under my nose. Her anger matched that of Antoine's.

"Mum, the big plate is horrible. Look at this pile of bones. There is no way I am eating that, it is just a pile of bones stuck into a soup," she said and added, "I have had enough of this awful party. I am going to bed." With that, she marched off into our house and closed the door.

True enough, the *big plate* was a disaster. It amounted to a big paella dish filled to the brim with a dark-coloured gravy, whereby if you inserted the scoop provided you could yield for yourself a bunch of cooked cheap offcuts of various types of meat, and if you were lucky, you could pull up something that you might recognise. In my case, I dipped the scoop in several times until I recognised two chicken legs. If it had not been for the large line of people behind me, I would have given the *big plate* a big miss, but I didn't want to appear rude. (*I Didn't Want to Appear Rude* would also have been a fitting title for this book.)

The story Simon told Antoine in what I could see was a rather heated discussion was that he had forgotten to buy rice, but as I had spotted several packets of rice by his stand earlier that day, how about he admitted that he was too drunk and had forgotten to put it in? That story would have been far more believable, especially if you had witnessed his bright red face, bulbous nose, beer belly and the obvious indicator, that of slurred speech. Case closed.

The birthday cake was a large rectangular one with a *Star Wars* theme. It had been placed on my kitchen table earlier in the evening to defrost and I had opened the cake box to peek in and reckoned that I could serve up to seventy people if I cut it into very small pieces. Candles had been provided and when the time was right, these were lit, and the cake was taken to the bar area where champagne was waiting to be served to wash down the cake. I had asked Thomas' girlfriend to start the rendition of *Bonne Anniversaire,* which shares the same tune as *Happy Birthday to You,* and everyone was soon joining in. Thomas was having the time of his life and was more than a few sheets to the wind as he blew out his candles. I noticed that the plastic champagne glasses had yet to have their stems attached and as I threw the box over to some unsuspecting person to rectify this *tout suite,* I walked back to the house to start the process of cutting up the cake.

It was an odd choice of cake as there was no pastry or sponge but instead it was of a white mousse consistency, and as I cut into it, there were parts that had still to defrost, which made it rather awkward to cut it evenly. It looked to be sitting on brown cardboard, which was a little odd considering that the whole cake was placed inside a large white cardboard box. I tried cutting down into the brown cardboard thinking that it may be some type of base, but it must have been frozen as I couldn't slice through it, and I didn't want to be serving up cake with something inedible attached to it, so I opted to leave it out. Some of the children had been sent in to help me to distribute the cake and as they came in to collect the slices two at a time, two of my helpers came running back. They attempted to explain that the cake was missing the base and as I did not understand, they pointed to the base and in a form of sign language they explained that the base was the best bit. Half of the cake had now been distributed and I couldn't very well chop up the base and ask the children to run around dropping off a piece of cake base, so since they deemed it to be the best bit, I broke it up into sections and gave it to them to do with as they deemed fit, which I guess was for them to eat it themselves. The rest of the cake, with the help of Marc, was cut up correctly and a large section with base was kept and presented to the birthday boy.

Once all the tables were cleared and plates stacked to one side, the volume was turned up and everyone got up to dance. We danced until the small hours of the morning and the party stopped when the bar was emptied. There was no tempting Beth out of her bed. Once something was deemed a write-off, it remained that way and she chose instead to put on her headphones to drown out the noise. It was her loss as the party did redeem itself, and by the time everyone went home, it was clear that they had all enjoyed themselves, Marc and I included.

With my Pollyanna brain, I had thought that the birthday party may have been a good opportunity for everyone to get together, but Clément and Laura and their two grown-up children, who were the cousins of birthday boy and of a similar age, had no intention of coming to the party and instead Clément chose to text me regularly on the build-up to the party to vent his anger towards me for getting involved. He was also angry at both of his parents for attending the party and for helping me to organise it. Clément offered me no explanation as to why we were not supposed to have a party or an explanation as to why he had no plans to attend; he simply did not want the party to go ahead. That in my mind and in the mind of his mother was not a valid reason.

With the party over and done with, Beth and I returned to our normal evenings of watching movies outdoors. The year previous, my brother had gifted us a projector and Marc had painted up a large sheet of white plywood and had hung it from a window attached to the storeroom next to our house. It was not uncommon for Antoine to come out to the garden, pull up a chair and watch a movie with us. We had gotten used to him gatecrashing our cinema evenings. I remember with great joy a particular evening when my two sisters and my father decided to fly out together to stay for the weekend. We had run through many options for a movie that Saturday evening and had finally picked *The Jazz Singer*. With sun loungers, cushions, blankets, and glasses filled to the brim with wine, we spent the evening singing our hearts out. Antoine's little face was a picture.

It wasn't long after the party that things took a sudden turn for the worse. It all started when the west wind blew in Antoine's ex-partner, Celine, and the mother of Thomas, back into his life, and into his life meant into ours too.

It was late one Saturday afternoon at the tail end of May when Marc was home when we noticed a people carrier pull up outside our kitchen window and a lady, who I guessed was in her late fifties, slightly stout with shoulder-length curly brown hair, exited the car. Her car was loaded to capacity with various household equipment, such as ironing boards, suitcases, folding chairs and step ladders, and one by one these were carried into the house. The next day, a small removal van pulled up, driven by a family friend, and the rest of her belongings were carried into the house. Antoine had rarely spoken about his ex as they had split up when Thomas was a toddler and we had just celebrated his thirtieth. She did not seem to be a part of his life, but then again, his son only started to visit when the pool was up and running. I had a feeling that his ex coming to stay was as much of a shock for Antoine as it was for those around him.

Strangely enough, Antoine was nowhere to be seen. Several weeks went by and whilst I saw this lady hanging out Antoine's denims and undies, he looked to be in hiding.

Mia explained on my next visit to pay the rent that Antoine did not appear to have a choice and that his ex had suddenly descended upon him with some story that she had nowhere else to go. The story seemed a bit hazy to Mia and she asked me to try to do a little digging if I was to speak with her or with Antoine. She was going to do the same from her side and had spoken to Clément to do the same so jointly we could figure out what was really going on.

A few days later and Clément had called in to speak with us about the latest news he had gleaned from his mother – that Celine's husband had died due to health complications caused by alcoholism. They had been living together for the last couple of years and had decided to quickly get married after they found out that he was not going to make it. After his death, the marriage made no odds to his children, who gave her her marching orders to leave the house and everything that belonged to their father as they strode in to claim their inheritance. It was a sad story and as she had walked out on Antoine numerous years ago, I thought it must have taken a large portion of humility for her to grovel her way back, but then again, she possibly felt it was her right. All credit to him, Antoine took her in, but then again, she did turn up with a car full to the brim of her belongings and claimed she had nowhere else to go, so I am unsure what choice he had.

Clément did not hide the fact that he didn't like Celine, which as usual came down to whether she was beautiful or not and, in this case, she was deemed to be a not.

Antoine had finally reappeared and had come over to enlighten me as to what was happening with the reappearance of his ex. He explained that he was not filled with joy about Celine's return but as the weeks had gone by, he found that he was beginning to enjoy her company and it helped that she had taken over the cooking. He didn't want to be seen to be taking advantage of her, so he continued to pay for his cleaner to come over. Madame Audrey was also his friend, who relied upon Antoine to listen to her grievances about her husband. There were many evenings when she would visit Antoine, drink a bottle of wine and drive herself home. Antoine was many things but a misogynistic bastard he was not and appeared to be the shoulder that could be relied upon as women vented their anger at being married to such a creature. Maybe he hoped one day that they would view him as more than a friend.

Antoine confided that his parents did not like Celine and were unhappy about her coming to stay, but that was to be expected. Mia made no secret of her role as head of her family despite Clément having a wife and children of his own, but in fairness to Mia on this occasion, she felt heart sorry for Celine and was supportive of Antoine taking her back in. I knew from one of Mia's stories that she too had found herself in a similar situation when one of her three husbands had left her for someone else.

For some reason or other, Celine's arrival after that seemed to increase Antoine's visits over to my house. He was now wandering over for morning coffee, coffee after lunch, and a final visit once he had finished work for a beer. Each visit was around an hour. It was awkward.

One day, I got caught up speaking to an Englishman and as we traded stories of our lives in France, he explained that he too had a neighbour who constantly visited them, and that he and his wife were at a loss as to how to get shot of him. I asked how they had finally managed it as he looked to be speaking about his neighbour in the past tense, and he announced with a laugh that fortunately his death had put an end to the visits.

"What age is your neighbour?" he asked.

"Mid-fifties," I replied. To which he laughed.

"You are going to have to wait a long time is my guess," he said, "unless of course you move house." He thought for a moment and added, "Probably best just to move house and not be so friendly with your neighbours the next time."

At the beginning of July, Beth and I were out for a swim when Celine came walking over to the pool to join us. Beth and I had been chatting at the deep end and we could see her walking over and perching herself at the base of the pool as she dangled her feet in the water. I quickly started to form some French sentences in my head as I swam my way down to chat with her. To my surprise, as I pulled up beside her, instead of a friendly chat, she announced very quickly that her family were coming down from Paris and that as this was her pool, she asked that we stop using it for the next three weeks as it was to be her family time.

There was nothing friendly about this lady but in her defence, I knew that she had been through a lot recently. She had made it clear that it was now her pool, so were her feet now firmly planted under Antoine's door? Were they a couple once more?

I had heard a lot of banging taking place on Antoine's roof that I had put down to repairs. A visit to Mia and she explained that Celine wanted to have a roof terrace installed so that she could sit outside her bedroom. Antoine did not have any money but had no hesitation in asking his mother. Wanting to be helpful and thinking that these two were now a couple, Mia was paying for the terrace but was displeased at the rising cost of it and questioned whether it was necessary. All the shenanigans were certainly giving the family a lot to talk about.

It was early July, and I was now in a situation whereby my neighbour's ex had asked me to quit using the pool for most of the month. We seldom used the pool now in August due to the amount of people coming to use it. What were we supposed to do?

When Antoine next strolled over to my house and sat on my wall, I was not the welcoming friendly Abi that he was expecting. The battery that stored my kindness and patience had officially run out and an *Empty* sign was placed around my neck. It was going to end badly, and I could not give two hoots.

"Antoine, I am fed up living in a public park. Celine has just informed me that I have not to use her pool for the next three weeks. I am fed up with you inviting people during the week and weekend and now the evenings to use the pool and the garden. I have no privacy. I pay to rent this house with the pool and to use the garden. You come to see me too often when it is my time with Beth. When Marc comes home, I will ask him to put a fence around my house and put a gate up. Your actions are causing a lot of stress in my house." I said all this slowly to ensure that he understood everything that I was saying. I was able to speak the majority of what I wished to say now in French and despite his screwed-up face that he put on when his ears had to tune into French with a Scottish accent, I could see that he understood every word as his face twisted and his eyes became fierce. I was letting out everything that I had sucked up over the past four years.

Silence, as he sat on my wall wondering what to do. He was angry and I could see that he had not expected me to confront him, because no one confronted Antoine; he manipulated everyone around him to ensure that he always got his way. He was still going to get his way. I was not stupid enough to doubt this and my outburst was going to be shared with all the family, the family that we had found ourselves unintentionally entangled with.

As I watched him, his face turned into that of a little boy, and he raised his hand to his heart and declared, "I cannot believe you say these things to me. You have broken me. It is *my* garden and it is *my* pool. Your house, it comes with only a terrace. You have no right to use this garden, it is mine. Your house, it is the house of *my* family, it is not your house. I ask who I want to *my* garden and *my* pool. You were like a sister to me, and you have broken my heart." With that, he stood up and proceeded to march back towards his house, stopping to turn with his hand still resting on his heart as he repeated the line, "You have broken my heart."

That was it. A phone call to Mum and they would all know that I had fallen out with their spoiled little brat. I was now in bad relations, most likely with all of them, because I was in no doubt that the blame would lie at my feet because that was by far the easiest option. There was to be no more kindness shown towards uninvited guests. There were to be no more visits from Antoine. I alerted Marc to the latest developments and we each knew that we now had no choice but to move house.

A few days later, Beth and I were each enjoying our *apero* as we sat by the little round table I had positioned by the pool. Beth and I were now opting to use the pool during mealtimes as the French are strict about what times they eat, and we were guaranteed to be left in peace. As I sat there quietly with Beth, sipping my glass of Crémant, I could hear that Antoine had his posse over and they too sounded like they were enjoying *apero* time. It was our favourite time of day; a time to relax and to discuss what we fancied eating for dinner and what movie we planned to watch that evening. We were having a few laughs about our life since moving to France and it was then that I heard Antoine's gate opening and saw Thomas' dog being ushered out.

This was not one of those friendly dogs that you could easily take to and ruffle its fur and have some fun with, no, this was a barky dog and one that would run around your feet time and time again. Sure enough, this little bundle of peskiness ran down towards us and as I reached out to shoo it away, my tipple toppled over on the table and the stem of my beautiful glass broke, a champagne coupe that I had recently purchased from an antique shop in the Alps. I looked at the dog and back to my glass and back to the dog. This was the final straw.

I reached down and grabbing the dog's collar I marched it up to Antoine's gate. Opening it, I saw his posse gathered around his terrace table. His son, Thomas, and his girlfriend, alongside Madame Audrey's daughter and her boyfriend.

"It is enough," I said as I made eye contact with each person around the table, who in their own way had pushed me to what was happening now. "It is rude to send your dog out to the garden. I pay to rent a house and to use this garden and to use the pool. Have you no respect? Take your dog and keep it here. You are very rude." Again, I said all of this in French. I wasn't shouting but I was firm and clear, but I also knew that none of these people had any respect for me or my family. In their eyes, it was Antoine's garden and pool and we were the uninvited guests.

As I walked out of the terrace and closed the gate, I could hear the gate opening again and watched as Thomas and his dog came out of the garden, walking towards me.

"You have no right to use this garden or pool," he said angrily to me. "The house you rent is my family house and you pay only to use the terrace." And with that he reached into his pocket and announced that he was phoning his grandmother (Mia).

I watched Thomas as he paced up and down the garden, shouting into his phone. I could make out that he was explaining that we had no right to use either the pool or the garden and he was also explaining that I had treated his dog badly. As he yelled and made an arse of himself, I recalled the time, work and money that I had put in to create for him a memorable birthday party and here he was just a few months later in the same garden, on the phone to his grandmother trying to get me evicted.

I knew from Mia that she did not have a good relationship with Thomas. She explained that he had been neglected by both of his parents and he had not been raised to have any form of relationship with his grandparents. She admitted that she did not like him. This was a tribal family, though, and he was family.

At long last, after much ranting and raving, he passed his phone over to me and announced in English, "It is your proprietor." I took the phone.

"Abi, what on earth is going on?" Mia asked. "I have just had Thomas speaking to me and he said that you have harmed his dog."

"Mia, I assure you that I did not harm his dog at all. I explained to you last year that our living situation here continues to deteriorate, and we are now looking for another house to rent. Your son and his family cause our family a lot of stress. They have zero respect for us renting your house. It was rude of Thomas to send his dog out into the garden this evening. I simply took the dog by its collar and led it up to Antoine's terrace," I explained calmly. I didn't mention the broken glass as after this fiasco it seemed like a trivial reason to have let rip.

"You know well what my son is like, Abi, and his son is not any better. We are in bad relations with him. I know well that he is not a good person, but he is my family and no matter what they do, I have to side with them. I am sorry, Abi, as I know they are in the wrong, but I can do nothing." Mia was reiterating what she had told me countless times. I was up against a tribe, and it was me against them.

They had indeed taken the whole arm. Antoine's jealousy ensured that no matter what we did, he imitated and gradually he took away everything.

The only option we now had was to leave. We had a problem, though. Marc had just applied to change his tax status as he went from entrepreneur to SARL (limited company), and whilst this was great news for our family's long-term future in France, for the moment it meant that we would have to wait a further two years to prove the success of the new business before we could rent a house from an estate agent.

We had few options, but life has always taught me that it is in these hopeless situations that if you think hard enough, a solution can be found. I was going to have to spend a lot of time thinking.

Ten

Clément

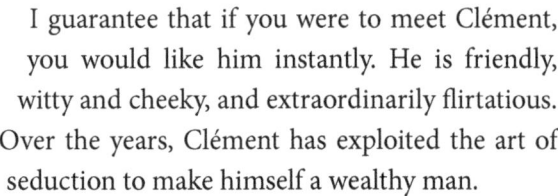

I guarantee that if you were to meet Clément, you would like him instantly. He is friendly, witty and cheeky, and extraordinarily flirtatious. Over the years, Clément has exploited the art of seduction to make himself a wealthy man.

If you were to walk into Clément's shop as a female, you would be sure to leave having bought something, such is his talent, and if you are male and arrive with a female, he will make you feel that you are the luckiest man in the world to have such a beautiful companion, and feeling so good about yourself, you will likely go onto make a purchase. He is good, bloody good.

Clément lives a very simple life and one not dissimilar to the one he had growing up when he worked at his parents' antique shop after school and during the weekends. Clément lives to work and in his spare time he loves to visit restaurants and to hunt. Clément is a self-confessed typical Frenchman; he hunts birds for his wife to make *pâté* and women for his own pleasure.

A 6am rise each morning to collect his two baguettes from his favoured *boulangerie,* which I hasten to add is two villages away because for one reason or another he is in bad relations with the ones situated nearby. Returning to his home for a breakfast consisting of half a baguette and jam washed down with four to five espressos followed by an abundance of smoke sticks courtesy of Philip Morris, and he is charged and ready to drive to work.

Clément manages the family antique shop that was supposedly entrusted to him when his father chose to retire several years ago. An ongoing problem, however, exists inasmuch as Jean-Baptiste does not like retirement, cannot let go of the reins and continues to buy antiques that have long since gone out of vogue, depositing them into Clément's shop, much to Clément's dismay. The once booming antique market in France continues to change, with clients becoming more selective, and whilst Jean-Baptiste and Mia could sell just about any old thing and make a substantial profit back in the day, there are now too many people in on the act, and it is my guess that a substantial amount of France's heritage has already been shipped overseas.

Clément loves to speak about the old times when the shop was at its busiest, but these days, as he sits and waits for potential buyers to arrive, or to receive a phone call from an overseas contact, he has a stack of time on his hands and he does what many French men do best...he switches on his laptop and contacts as many women as he can with the hope that his wife does not catch him out. His wife, he admits, often catches him out despite him using his favoured social network, Facebook, which allows him to act out under various aliases.

There was a charming and witty side to this man but from his occasional confessions and sexist comments, I was beginning to see there was possibly a darker side.

His wife and his daughter, he declared, watched his every move, and it was common for Clément to proclaim:

"*Je suis comme un lion en cage.*"

Personally, having known Clément for several years, I question the animal he relates to and instead I would compare him to a French Bulldog with behavioural problems, on one side appearing well tempered and friendly, suffering from separation anxiety when he has the necessity to leave his area or those that he feels comfortable around, and having a darker nature fuelled by jealousy that allows him to gain his strength from speaking badly to and of the female race. I would most certainly agree with the cage part as there is no man more restricted in his behaviour than Clément.

Clément was raised in an environment where his mother carved out for herself, and continues to hold, the role of matriarch. A strict upbringing where his parents never learnt to let go, as seems to be the case in a tribal family, continuing to parent someone who towards the end of this book himself became a grandfather. Everyone had control issues in this family, and each was manipulative in their own way. Mia has made it abundantly clear that she remains the head of her family and will hold this role until she dies. She telephones each of her boys several times a day with any news and to find out what is happening in their lives. Considering it is a rare event for any of them to travel far, I am unsure how the conversation could possibly go. Never did I hear any stories about holidays or trips to the beach or a skiing vacation for that matter; it was just a repeat of daily life from one week to the next. There was, however, the topic of new restaurants and the usual village gossip, two topics that are on the lips of most village-bound people, I would imagine, a chat that could likely take up a couple of hours or so each day.

Mia has even gone as far as to buy a family funeral plot, where her mother presently resides, and has a place reserved for herself, her husband, Antoine and Clément. There are no additional spaces reserved for the family of either Antoine or Clément. What keeps these boys toeing the line? This is aptly summed up with the French saying, *La carotte est suspendue devant l'âne* (the carrot is suspended before the donkey), the carrot being their forthcoming inheritance.

Since I have known this family, the word *inheritance* seems to have cropped up in every sentence. Every topic can relate somehow to what is going to happen when their parents die and they receive their inheritance. It is like listening to a drunk propping up a bar and speaking to his friend about his plans for how he is going to spend his money when he wins the lottery. The French inheritance is clearly a way for parents to keep in control of their children.

What Clément expresses as 'typical' around these parts was getting together with a local girl at a very young age and having children early. He sighed, "That's just what we all did back then." We knew that to be true because in all the years we knew this man, he told us the same two stories repeatedly about something that happened when he was single. I have opted to exclude the stories down to their lack of interest, and I can only think that his repeating them was to indicate, "See, I did have a life prior to getting married." Did he, though?

Clément chose to marry a farmer's daughter, which in these parts can unfortunately be classed as marrying a peasant, a term that can often be used in a derogatory way. This girl was strong, she knew what she wanted and according to Jean-Baptiste, she stole his son. Jean-Baptiste and his daughter-in-law loathe each other 364 days of the year, but on Christmas day they manage to tolerate each other for the sake of Mia.

Trapped between two headstrong women, Clément tends to accept his fate, but from time to time he erupts.

In year two, around Easter time, a very wound-up Clément called in to have morning coffee with us.

"That is it!" he announced as he walked down the stairs onto our terrace. "I cannot be with that woman any longer. I tell her today it is finished."

It wasn't unexpected as Marc had heard from Antoine that Clément had gone ahead and purchased a puppy without consulting his wife. His wife seemingly was mad and gave him the ultimatum, "It is the dog or me." And the story goes that he chose the dog.

As Clément drank his coffee, he confirmed the story of the dog and the fact that as he had chosen the dog as a preferred companion, his wife had packed up and gone to her mother's.

"I go back with that woman, never again." He confirmed, "This time, it is over."

True enough, a week or so later I had gone to pay our rent and Mia confirmed that Clément and Laura had split up. She was not surprised and added that they had split up numerous times before, but that this time it was finished, and they were to go for a divorce.

Several weeks passed by and the next we heard was from Antoine, who came over to tell us that whilst Clément was at work, his wife had come back to the house and had packed up all his belongings and kicked him out. Clément was now living with his parents.

Several more weeks passed and they were at it again, with Clément moving back in and with his wife moving back to her parents'. Clément had texted both Marc and I to tell us that they were meeting with a lawyer to divide up their estate.

A week or so later, I received a text from Clément to say that they had decided to get back together because he realised that he loved his wife. The real version of the story came from Antoine, who after speaking with his mother learnt that his wife was going to fight for half of everything, including his stack of cash. He had also found himself cooking and cleaning for himself and felt a lesser man for not having a woman to clean up after him, although he had employed a lady to wash and iron his clothes.

As the seasons passed, Clément got into a habit of texting both Marc and I. We all seemed to genuinely hit it off but from time-to-time Clément would throw around derogatory and blatantly sexist comments about women with the obvious intention of winding me up. I have never found it easy in these situations as if you say something as a female, you are considered too sensitive, and if you say nothing, they feel they can step it up. I find it hard to know if it is banter or if it is designed to be hurtful. I suppose that is the idea. I was surrounded by similar men when I went shopping and opted to put it down to poor behaviour caused by low self-esteem rather than simply an issue with Clément himself.

Clément had suggested to Marc not long after we had moved into his father's house to call into his shop when he needed some money, as often he needed a hand to lift a heavy item or just wanted company to deliver purchased antiquities. At 10€ an hour, it was slave labour, but it was a little pocket money and it gave Marc the opportunity to see other villages and to meet new people as well as stopping for the obligatory French lunch, paid for by Clément. Marc was sure to relate the day's events in the accent of Clément, which was guaranteed to have Beth and I in stitches.

"Marc, look, see that woman there. She is not beautiful but many years ago she was beautiful."

"That woman there, look, she has the big breasts."

"The woman who flirt with me, these are the woman of stupid."

"I have a lot of women contact me on Facebook for a relation. I do not like that. I love my wife."

Marc used to wonder if he had the words *wife* and *life* confused when he was attempting to learn English, other than the fact that neither made any sense.

On one occasion as they were driving through Avignon, Clément was in a hurry to drive up beside a car that had been in front of them for some time.

"Marc, see this lady in front, she is beautiful, I smell it," he said as he tapped his nose.

Upon pulling up to the car, he leaned over to Marc's side to look out of the window and Marc of course looked too as at this stage he thought Clément knew the driver and wanted to speak with her. Instead, as the startled woman turned around to look at the two men rudely peering at her, Clément chose his time to make an announcement.

"No, she is not beautiful," he said as he shook his head whilst looking at her.

Keeping in mind the lady also had her window down, Marc was sure she had heard his comment and was sure to have heard the laughter that followed.

It was not as if he had anything good to say about his wife.

"My wife, she wears the pantaloon, why she not wear the robe? I 'ate zat."

"My wife, she do nothing. She plays games on the computer all day. I 'ate zat."

"My wife, she looks at my phone and she check my computer to see who I talk to. I 'ate zat."

"My wife, she does not like that I help other people. She says I must stop to be kind. I 'ate zat."

"My wife, she does not like my parents. I 'ate zat."

"My wife is a very jealous woman. I 'ate zat."

"My wife, she interferes all the time with the lives of our children. You must do that, you must not do that. I 'ate that she does that. It does not matter that they have left the house. She still phones them every day and interferes in their lives all the time. I 'ate zat."

"My wife, I tell her, Laura, you are fat and she says, no, you are fat and I say it is true, I am fat, but it is okay for a man to be fat, it is not good for a woman. Since then, she has gone to swim every day and now she is not fat. I am happy of zat."

Clément came across as a very frustrated man.

Clément was also the local self-appointed restaurant critic. As they drove along, he would often point over to each restaurant to give Marc the low-down.

"That one, the proprietor, he not come to say hello to me when I go to his restaurant. I 'ate zat."

"That one, it is too much expensive."

"That one, I know a man who says you do not get enough food for what you pay, so I do not go."

"That one, it is good, very good. It is my favourite."

"That one, someone in the family of my wife owns it, so you must go. You must go all the time."

We often sensed that Clément enjoyed our company because he saw himself as rich and us as poor, and I would think at times whilst he sat with us over a few beers boasting about how much money he was making and how it was doubtful that we would ever earn more than 2,000€ per month (talk about a stuck record), that if I were to draw a cartoon of Clément at that moment, it would be that of a slightly pot-bellied peacock, and instead of a spread of feathers, it would be a spread of euros. The peacock would of course be smoking a cigarette.

One day, an opportunity arose for us to finally meet Clément's wife. In truth, neither of us was looking for an opportunity and would have let this one slip if we could have, given her reputation, but we were kind of roped in because Clément made out that when members of two different families decide to work together, it is customary for the families to meet up and share a meal. This could be a French tradition, or he could just have made it up, who knows, but we didn't want to appear rude, so agreed. Marc had texted and given Beth and I twenty minutes' notice. Not great when you are preparing for a lazy day by the pool.

The restaurant took Beth and me by surprise because it was situated in the middle of a business park and not somewhere where we expected to find a restaurant. As we walked into the main entrance, it was rather charming, and walking through the main dining area took us down to a beautiful decked terrace surrounded by trees, where we found Marc and Clément waiting for us as they sat at a table under the royal blue sky. As we settled in, a woman approached and stood by our table and Clément introduced her as his wife, Laura. She was taller than her husband, of medium build, free of any make-up and, without being unkind, skin, teeth and a voice that indicated a long and heavy addiction to cigarettes. It was a common look in Provence and one that did not embody the world's view of French women but one that did explain why the French produce such a vast array of expensive skincare products. She had dark brown shoulder-length hair and was wearing an ensemble of an old tee-shirt teamed up with a bobbly pair of slacks finished off with a pair of Scholl's. Considering Clément's obsession with who was beautiful and who was not, she was not the trophy wife that I had expected. She had a sour expression, and it was clear that she did not want to be eating with us. As she took her seat across from Beth, I wondered if she had parked her car or if she had instead flown in on her broomstick. I decided not to ask the question as I didn't know the word *broomstick* in French, and it would have been rude to spend time on Google translating at this early part of the lunch.

Beth was not in the best of moods either, as she had her heart set on spending the afternoon in the pool and it had taken a lot of persuasion for her to come with me. When Laura positioned herself across from Beth with her clearly unhappy disposition, it did not make for a happy scene and Beth started to sob.

With some clear eye contact around the table, it was apparent that with the arrival of Madame Misery-guts, this was not likely to be an enjoyable lunch, so collectively we made the decision to skip entrées to speed things up. As lunch proceeded, Beth, who had started off just sobbing quietly, was now gearing up and her crying was becoming louder and louder. She was seriously pissed off. It did not help that Laura kept looking at Beth and up at me in a manner that insinuated that I should be sorting out my 'naughty' child, failing to take into consideration that Beth was happy until she had placed herself directly across from her. The lunch just went from bad to worse with each subject and reached a very awkward moment as it led to where Marc and I had met and how soon thereafter we had tied the knot. I explained that we met and married within four months of meeting each other, which was met with a scowl from Laura (a more pronounced scowl than the one she arrived with).

"It took six years for him [she said, pointing with her thumb at Clément] to marry me and he did not want to." She spoke to us in French as Clément translated. As he did so, he laughed.

"It is true," said Clément. "I did not want to marry but I do for the tax."

Awkward silence as Laura sat shaking her head at her husband as he returned to eating his lunch.

Continued awkward silence and a terrific opportunity to use Beth as an excuse to get out.

As Beth and I walked out of the restaurant for a saunter around the business park, her mood completely brightened as she saw her opportunity to go home and finally jump in the pool. It is unfortunate, I explained, that in these adult situations when everyone is having lunch, you cannot just up and leave as it would be deemed to be rude; however, if she was prepared to help me, we could return, finish lunch and leave quickly. Like her mother, she was up for playing a game if it was deemed necessary.

When we returned to our seats, the conversation was still about marriage, and Laura was explaining to Marc that Clément never remembered their wedding anniversary.

"Can you remember the date?" she barked at Clément in French.

"No, I am not interested in things like zat," he said, laughing.

As I watched them closely, I could see that she was visibly hurt, and he was clearly enjoying seeing her so.

The subject of marriage was not going away as she went onto remove her wedding band to show us the inside of the ring, which was inscribed with both their names and the date of their marriage, and as she did so, he continued to laugh as he waved it away. The more he laughed, the more upset she appeared, to the point where I thought she was going to get up and leave, but instead she quietly went back to finishing her lunch.

It was a great relief when everyone had eaten up, as Beth had been primed that with a gentle tap on her leg she was to start crying again and this was to be our chance to escape…for good this time.

That was all in year one, and in year two, with Marc spending around twenty-five days per month in the Alps, Clément seemed keen to continue to call in and on at least two occasions he called in to ask me for my telephone number even though he had been occasionally texting me. I was reluctant to give him my telephone number when he initially asked for it, and I found it bizarre that he was asking me for my number again. I did not want to get myself into trouble with his wife and I wondered what kept happening to my number. When he asked me for my number for the third time, I was hesitant, but he explained that with Marc being away for several weeks per month, it was good for me to have someone close by in case there was an emergency of any kind. Fair point.

Several months had passed and it was a very cold winter, so much so that there was a light covering of snow on the ground. Marc had chopped up some firewood, which he deemed to be more than enough until his next visit, but unfortunately it wasn't, and we ran out. I couldn't ask Antoine because he had a pellet burner, therefore no firewood. I spoke with Marc, and he suggested that I text Clément as he always had old offcuts of wood at his shop and that likely I could just call in and load up.

Instead of texting Clément, I called into see him and told him of my predicament, enquiring as to whether he had any old offcuts lying around that would serve me until Marc made it home. The response was not what I had expected, as he told me that he did not like it when a woman asked for something from him and that it was Marc's responsibility to look out for me, not his. Nonetheless, he stacked up my boot with old wood and later that evening he came around with his van and offloaded a load more.

"I 'ate when people ask me for something. I want that people like me for me and not for what I can give to them," he said abruptly before stepping back into his van and driving off.

When Marc returned and called in to see Clément, he received an unexpected lecture about how he had not taken care of his family and how I had turned up at his shop asking him for wood when we were Marc's responsibility and not his. Marc too was put out by his reaction, and on that visit, Marc made sure to have chopped up enough firewood to last us several winters.

To keep relations sweet so that we were not on the 'bad relation list', I took Clément a bottle of whisky to say thank you for the wood. He was sure to speak to his family about his gift so I opted to buy a bottle for Jean-Baptiste as well as Antoine as, in that way, the gift should cover anything that they felt I may have overlooked.

As the months went by and funny texts were being circulated about one thing or another, Marc and I felt that we could include Clément as a friend and Marc went as far as to suggest that we take Clément and Laura out for lunch. It wasn't the greatest suggestion that Marc had ever come up with but with Clément having given Marc work previously, and seeing that Clément was a very sensitive individual who did not like to be taken advantage of, it made sense for Marc to shout lunch now that he was in a better financial position to do so, keeping in mind that a lunch in France for four people can easily come to 150-200€, which is a lot to shell out when finances are tight.

On this occasion, we opted to meet in a village that was famed for its abundance of antiques. We had no wish to repeat the events of the last lunch. Clément seemed to know a lot of people as we made our way to the restaurant, stopping to exchange a fair amount of *bisous*.

Finally, a little later than anticipated, we followed Clément and Laura as they took us down a few windy lanes before we reached a small restaurant tucked behind a shop. Neither Marc nor I would ever have found this place, so it was nice to be with people who were familiar with the best places to eat. There were people sitting outside and whilst it was a sunny day, there was a cool breeze and none of us were keen to sit out, so headed indoors to be seated. The owner directed us to a cosy area adjacent to the bar, with Laura and Clément opting to sit with their backs to the wall, allowing them to face the entrance and to see people coming in, whilst Marc and I sat facing them with our backs to the door. Our only view that afternoon was these two, what joy! As we each sat perusing the menu, we heard the restaurant door opening.

"*Salut*, Clément," I heard a female say in a very flirtatious tone.

Clément looked up, eyes wide, and put his head down quickly as he mumbled, "*Salut*."

She continued to direct her attention and conversation to Clément, who at this point had lifted his menu up to his face as he pretended to be studying it. I guessed from his shocked expression that he was hoping the ground was going to open and swallow him whole.

"This is my wife," I heard him say as he lowered his menu and cut the woman off mid-sentence.

I had no idea what the lady had been saying to Clément, but when I looked at Laura's face, she was livid.

The lady laughed.

I looked over at Laura, who seemed desperate to speak but was finishing off a piece of toasted baguette topped with tapenade that the owner had placed on our table as we sat down. Finally, she looked up at the lady and muttered something sharply as she shook her head whilst looking from the lady to Clément and back to the lady again. I could hear the woman laughing nervously as I looked across at Clément, whose head was still inside his menu. There was a brief silence until I heard the door open and close behind me as she made her exit, and with her gone, Laura turned to Clément and muttered something under her breath. I did not know what she had said but it was clear that it was not something endearing. That was the start of our second lunch with these two delightful individuals.

We ordered our food and as I looked over at Clément, the smile that had formed after Laura had given him a piece of her mind remained on his face. Clément the *séducteur* had struck again, and it was obvious to Marc and me that he was in his element and loving every minute of this. I looked over to Marc and smiled. In truth, I wanted to laugh out loud as these two were a disaster together. It was like watching a very naughty schoolboy being caught out by his mother.

As lunch progressed, I pulled my list out of my handbag. I called my list Plan B, a list of safe subjects that could be used if the conversation became too personal and uncomfortable. In this instance, I had opted to write down some French slang words that I had found in a French book that I was reading. As I went through my list of words and jotted down their responses, I could see Laura start to smile as she patiently explained their meanings.

This was going well. As I continued with my list of words, I could see a twinkle appear in Clément's eyes as he interrupted what I was about to say next.

"I like your hair like that, Abi," he said. "I like the way it is around your face. It is good like that. You must keep it like that."

I glared at Clément in a half joking, half what-the-hell-are-you-doing kind of way. His face was as mischievous as I had ever seen it, and I cottoned on that he was using me to wind up his wife. There was no love lost between these two. For me, in my head, this was not a real situation but instead a comedy sketch where Marc and I were sitting with a stereotypical randy Frenchman and his stereotypical jealous wife, and they were both playing their parts incredibly well. A César award was in the bag.

I remained smiling at his childish antics and shaking my head, I happened to look over to Laura, who was sitting across from Marc. She had stopped eating, had placed her cutlery down on the table and had leaned back on her chair as she stared at me, narrowing her eyes with an expression that without doubt said go near my husband and I will kill you, or something as threatening as that, maybe without the death part, but I could not be certain.

With our current relationship with Antoine deteriorating, I knew that we had no choice but to move house. I also knew that Clément owned a rental house with its own pool, situated in a very desirable little village that I was familiar with. I had a feeling that I needed to reply to his texts whether I wished to or not. It was a risk I considered, at the time, worth taking.

Eleven

The seducer, the predator & the spider

A popular British comedy once cracked the joke that a Frenchman would shag the kitchen sink if it was wearing a tutu. Another joke from the same show suggested that the greatest French invention was self-removing trousers.

Frenchmen have gotten themselves quite the reputation and indeed when Beth brings home her French books and learns the history of famous French poets such as Victor Hugo and Charles Baudelaire, for example, the invention of the self-removing trousers seems to go back to at least the mid 1800s.

As for shagging the kitchen sink if it was wearing a tutu, I would say that if a Frenchman was presented with the opportunity, he would firstly give it a good look-over, decide what age it was, look for flaws, bring these flaws to the attention of the kitchen sink and if they were lucky enough to be let out of their cage for just a minute, they would most likely give it their best attempt. A minute, after all, is likely to be more than adequate.

Having worked in various office environments in the UK, I was more than aware of the seduction games that had to be played at times in order to climb the professional ladder but as a nation we weren't the most flirtatious in our daily lives, and flirting tended to stay within the work environment or after a few drinks in the pub. In France, it is rumoured that seduction is a part of everyday life and to some extent that is true as there always seems to be someone ready to pounce whilst walking down the street, ordering your croissants at your local *boulangerie*, waiting in a queue at the supermarket, by a supermarket employee, when going in to service your car and whilst enjoying a coffee at a local café. It bodes well to familiarise yourself with the French art of seduction.

When we arrived in France, we had put together a to-do list. On our initial list, remaining at the top for some time was opening a bank account. Marc and I had tried and failed on several occasions because we did not have a current utility bill and they would not accept an alternative to this. How were we supposed to get one when we were living in a holiday rental?

After much discussion with Marc, it occurred to me that for us to secure a bank account, we were going to have to be a good bit more French in our ways, i.e., one of us was going to have to seduce a bank account out of someone. Either Marc was to wear his finest and go heavy handed on the aftershave or I was to do the female equivalent and maybe then we could get what we wanted. This was the French way after all. Marc and I made the deal that we would each do what we had to do, with one strict criterion – whatever we did had to benefit the family.

Marc has many talents, but flirting is most certainly not one of them, so the decision was made that I was to become the *séductrice*, and I was very much looking forward to playing my new role.

Dressed in smart but casual and wearing my finest black high-heeled leather boots, a splash and a half of Chanel No. 5, make-up on and hair styled, in French city chic, I was ready to cross my bank account off the list.

As I walked into my soon-to-be bank, I apologised in my blonde and naïve manner for my poor French and was it possible that there was someone available that I could speak to that spoke a little English? A phone call was made and as I passed the time in the waiting area, a tall and very distinguished man, a touch younger than I, approached me to ask if I would come up to his office to see if he could help me. So far, so good.

It was a small office and as he sat down behind his desk and I took a seat across from him, I had the distinct impression that the universe had beamed this one down for me. He had dark hair, quite distinct green eyes and a healthy complexion. He was a charmer for sure and as he spoke to me in English, I could see by his manner that he was extremely proud to be speaking English with his exaggerated French accent. I complimented him on his fluency and the fact that the Queen of England would undoubtedly be impressed. As we spoke together, I could see that we were both now playing the same game. We chatted for some time about the countries in which he had travelled and from there to why I had moved over to France. I praised his country for its magnificent climate, food and particularly for the very handsome and courteous Frenchmen that I enjoyed speaking with, such as himself. I sighed, smiled and made sure that the leg I had crossed was pointing in his direction.

"You are married?" he asked as he leaned back on his chair, to which I nodded.

"How unfortunate and I should warn you that this is going to be a typical line from a Frenchman when he wants to get to know you. What is it that you would like for me to assist you with?"

I explained that I had been recommended to his bank by some of our new French friends and that we were looking to open a bank account. He explained that he would need to see our passports, birth and marriage certificates, statements from our previous bank in the UK as well as a recent utility bill. I was going to have to turn up the heat for the last one.

"I have all of these here," I said as I handed them over to him, "but I cannot provide you with a utility bill because we are living in holiday accommodation and our rent covers the electricity and water." I paused, sighed, played with my hair before continuing. "Can you think of a way around this because I would really like to use your bank?"

He leaned back on his leather swivel chair and stared at me as I returned the eye contact of what I could be prepared to do if I got what I came for. He looked down to what I had handed him and proceeded to read through all our documents.

"I have your marriage certificate here. Can you remember what date you were married?" he asked coyly.

It was a test; I knew it. "Oh, that is one date I always forget, let me think for a moment. It was October, no, it was November, and the date, oh, I always get the date mixed up between the 11th and the 16th. I am going to go with [pause, playing with hair] the 16th of November."

He laughed. "I am going to be sure to tell your husband of our conversation."

Note to self – explain the conversation to Marc so he can be prepared and have the right response should this subject be raised on our next visit.

"I think there is a way," he said, seemingly happy with all our documents. "If you ask your proprietor for a letter addressed to me that states that the rent you are paying includes the electricity and water, I will make an exception for you."

"Wow, thank you so much," I replied, genuinely elated. "I will ask my proprietor today and will call you to make a second rendezvous."

As I got up to leave, he asked me to sit back down as he was going to photocopy something to give to me. As he returned and gave me the list of what he required, I got up to leave a second time and this time he stood by the door to block my entrance.

"I am trying desperately to think of something else so that you can stay in my office for longer," he said as he looked longingly into my eyes. It was at this point that I had a flashback to an old Doris Day and Rock Hudson movie and inwardly I was laughing as I thought about the chances of this type of encounter happening at the Bank of Scotland. It took everything within me to hold myself together to stop myself from laughing. Remaining in character and calling up Doris in my mind allowed me to reply.

"I will return soon, I promise, and I look forward to it very much."

With that, I said my goodbyes and made my way downstairs and out of the bank. Outside the bank there was a large florist shop and I had stopped for a moment to look at the beautiful window displays, and as I was walking away, I heard someone running behind me and shouting my name. As I turned around, to my surprise, there stood Monsieur Banque.

"I forgot to give you this," he said as he handed me over a form that he could easily have given to me on my next visit.

"It is the day of Saint Valentine today. Is your husband going to buy you flowers?" he asked as we both looked over towards the flower shop.

"Oh, I doubt that," I replied as I laughed. "He is a New Zealander, so there is little chance I will be receiving anything."

"If I knew you better, I would buy you flowers." And with that he gazed into my eyes momentarily before walking slowly back into the bank.

This was truly a French movie moment, and I must be honest and say that it was quite sensual. I had been married a fair while by now and my flirting skills were rusty, or so I had thought, but his technique, wow, it was at a whole new level. If I opted to use seduction to secure what I wanted, I realised that I was going to find myself in a whole heap of trouble.

It is fair to say that Marc was happy with the news that I had secured a bank account and agreed that my methods were working. Upon our return visit, Monsieur Banque did mention to Marc that I had forgotten the date of our anniversary and Marc laughed. "That sounds like Abi," he replied as we gave each other the knowing look. I could see that Monsieur Banque was enjoying flirting with me in front of Marc.

Our bank account was set up and we had received our cards and I was very happy with the service, emailing the bank to say so. I had forgotten about Monsieur Banque after that until one day I received an email out of the blue from him, asking if I needed any help with learning French and would I like to meet up with him? I read my email out to Marc, to which he responded:

"It sounds okay, Abi, as we are going to need a mortgage at some point and you being friends with him may just help." Was he serious or joking? We looked at each other and laughed. I sent my response, thanking him and explaining that I was receiving lessons from someone else and thanked him again for his help. A few weeks after that, I received an email from the bank to say that Monsieur Banque had moved location and I now had a new bank manager, for which I was relieved. Maybe he had moved banks or maybe he had gone into movies; the second option I felt would have suited him far better.

Frenchmen as a rule are hugely confident with women, but I found them very divided in their approach. There exists *le séducteur,* a confident and well-dressed individual who isn't always handsome but knows how to dress, how to style his hair, has impeccable manners and most importantly has learnt how woman tick. My ex-bank manager certainly fitted into this category. With foreign women, they know at times that by exaggerating their accent, it is enough to win them over... in a jiffy, they tell me. Sometimes, they will discreetly speak with you in the street as you shop, often making an excuse to ask for directions, leading to an invitation to share a drink. At times, they can persuade the waiter to approach you to gain their attention. Or the man behind the counter of the *boulangerie* who catches your eye when you enter and looks for any excuse to serve you and takes his time wrapping up each item you have purchased as he makes eye contact, indicating that more than patisseries are on offer. If you have the need to turn down a request from these gentlemen, there tends not to be any bitterness or unkindness on their part as they know that there exists plenty of women out there who are more worthy of them. These men have a high opinion of themselves, and flirting is a hobby that should never be treated seriously on the part of the female unless of course they are unattached. If attached and you are looking for a 'quickie', they most likely have a very limited time off their lead, so time is of the essence.

Sadly, there exists not such a nice version: *le prédateur*. One that tracks you down only to speak mean and to cause you hurt. These men have learnt the patter of *le séducteur* but they look to be at the opposite end of the self-esteem spectrum, and with nothing to lose and undoubtedly hating their lives, no sooner have they complimented you to pull you into their snare than it is closely followed by something belittling or sexist.

One sunny afternoon whilst walking through the back end of a market in Aix-en-Provence, a man who was working at one of the stalls approached me and stood in front of me to ensure that I came to a halt. As he started to speak with me, his eyes slowly travelled up and down my body and rested on my face. As he finished speaking, I explained that I spoke very little French as I had only just arrived in France. That did not seem to be an issue as he responded by holding one of his hands up to his face just below his nose where he held it horizontally and responded in English.

"I only want to tell you that I prefer the top half of your face to the bottom half."

And with that he stared at me coldly and walked off. I was taken aback but when someone says something mean, I tend to make allowances and, on this occasion, it was not difficult for me to do so because this man was neither blessed with good looks nor the ability to dress well, and he was clearly very unhappy with his life. Speaking to me simply to convey something mean looked to be his method of feeling good about himself that day. Misogyny is a much talked-about problem in France.

Whilst shopping at my local supermarket one day, I was approached by one of the male workers who walked right up to me and started to whisper something in my ear. It was not something that I had expected, and not knowing what he had said made it almost impossible for me to respond. I didn't want to overreact if he was for that matter pointing out that if I was to purchase two packets of what I was holding, I would get the third one free, but I doubted that was worth whispering, so I did my usual and responded that I only spoke a small amount of French. I could have complained because this happened on a further two occasions by other members of staff, but how do you complain when you cannot understand all of what is being said and, of course, there was always the likelihood of one of the culprits being the manager himself.

The longer I lived in Provence, the more bizarre I tended to find the people, and, in all honesty, I have to say that the French down these parts have an uncanny way of making married life look insufferable. The relationship between the sexes does not look to have changed since the 1950s, or possibly the 1850s, or maybe never at all. Men are raised to be 'macho' and a woman looks to be classed as either the strong/replacement mother type or the beautiful/hunting material type. I have never spent time analysing the relationship between a man and a woman before, but there have been times since living here that I have disliked being a woman, and I wanted to find out what was going on.

Ageing seems to have a peculiar effect on many married couples in these parts. It doesn't take long to find an example, because they are everywhere; it is a simple case of walking into any supermarket with your eyes open. Upon entering, you will without doubt see a couple, the man normally pushing the trolley and the wife loading it up. As the wife loads up, her husband is scanning the shop looking for anyone that does not resemble his wife. The problem is that as he looks around, most women do resemble his wife, such are the hard lives these women look to have had. As he scans, his wife looks on now and again with a scowl which increases when his gaze is halted by someone that does not resemble her and is a few decades younger. I will stop at this point to offer some advice.

If you are female and are approaching such a couple, and they are impossible to miss, you should try your utmost to avoid eye contact. Look down to the ground, look up to the ceiling, but avoid looking in their direction. If you choose to ignore this piece of advice and chance it, you can play the game of counting to three. One, two, and on the count of three, the husband will have had the few seconds required to think up a way to get your attention as he combines his creepy chat with his beady eyes that look to be undressing you slowly. If you are unfortunate enough to be fluent in French, be prepared for an initial kind comment followed by something not so kind. This process seems to give these poor creatures some perverse pleasure. If that is not bad enough, you will now have vengeance poured upon you by the wife, who will have watched her husband prepare for the encounter and watches as he purrs over you. Be thankful that her eyes do not contain lasers because at this point you would surely be cut in half.

What the hell was going on? Why did Provence have so many couples who behaved in this manner?

Beth was always a good person to ask as she was equally as observant and opinionated as her mother and was intrigued by the behaviour of others. Beth informed me that when she started *collège*, which was located within a very small village, the children were constantly approaching her to ask why she was here. They found village life boring, they informed her, and many of them wanted out at the first opportunity, so why would someone voluntarily come from the UK to live here? It made no sense to them and when Beth used to come home to repeat the question that she herself found no words to answer, I at times struggled myself to find an explanation. "To get away from everything so that we could simply be ourselves" was the answer that I stuck with because that was ultimately what was working for us all. Beth may have been bored at times, but she was not bullied or questioned in the manner she was subjected to in her school in the UK. She was never judged. These children lived a simple life, went to school in any apparel that they felt comfortable in, and lived the way children should live without unnecessary pressure.

As these children grew up, though, I started to wonder what hopes and dreams were put to them and from whom? Within Beth's education, we saw a big difference between the attitude of the teachers from the international school as opposed to the teachers from the *collège*. Reaching for the stars, being proud to be yourself and being encouraged not to be a sheep was promoted well at her initial school but from the time that she moved into public French schooling, that side of things looked to be passed over as teachers had a more distant relationship with the children. It seemed to me that they were concentrating on churning out children born from previous children that had attended, with the thought process maybe that nothing was ever going to change around these parts. I could understand therefore why many French families were choosing to put their children into international schools. Beth was happy to stick it out as there wasn't much asked of her and she was happy for a free ride. She is a very confident girl and was not relying upon the school's encouragement to reach for the stars, because in Beth's mind as soon as school life was over with, she was off travelling. Settling down with a French boy and living in a French village with a mother-in-law in range was and still is Beth's idea of hell.

It is common here when asking how someone's nephew or son is getting on at school to hear the father or uncle refer to them proudly as being 'macho'. It was not an expression that I ever heard being used in the UK; therefore, I thought I would do some research on it.

The French macho image, according to some historians, goes back to the abundance of strong male characters in French history, leaders and fighters, writers and poets who had their fair share of wives and mistresses and lived predominately pleasing themselves. French history does not have the same abundance of strong female characters and, for the most part, French men still like to hunt and collect females as they attempt to feel strong and dominant towards the other half whilst living at home with their replica mothers. Girls continue to be raised as men pleasers. I understand why many women have claimed the 'matriarch' title as they force out for themselves a role that makes them feel strong. I question, though, whether this strength of character could be put to better use by encouraging their daughters to seek adventure, holding out the hope that there exists more to a French girl's life than leaving school, grabbing the first man that comes along and making babies.

Why are predators so prevalent in Provence? An inadvertent tongue twister. To get to the bottom of this, I spoke to a wide range of people, gently raising the subject to obtain their opinions.

I was told by some of the younger men that they felt French women were spider-like in their approach to finding a man and that they knew of too many men who had been trapped through pregnancy into a long-term relationship and that maybe this created the problem. These women, they said, just wanted children and any man would do. One man in his early thirties offered, "If a French woman tells me that sex is better without a *préservatif*, I put on two." When I mentioned this comment to Clément, who was in his late forties, his response was "Ooff, contraception is the job of the woman. It is not for the men to use the *préservatif*." I thought about their different responses and how the younger man was happy and free living with a British girl, discussing whether they wished to have children rather than the woman making the decision on her own, whereas Clément's dated approach to birth control perhaps allowed him to be caught. The younger man had respect for his girlfriend and treated her as his equal, whereas Clément felt he was superior to women.

A belief also seems to be held by some that it is better to select a strong woman as opposed to a beautiful one. The reasoning appears to go along the lines that beautiful women do not want to work and will be too busy thinking about themselves to spend the time raising a family and caring for all the needs of their husband. Beautiful women also attract other men; therefore, it is safer to keep an unattractive woman at home, treating them mean to keep them keen and going out to hunt down the beautiful woman that you intend to treat in the same questionable manner. The Frenchman's thought process looks to be: "Why can't a man have both bread and wine and not prefer one before the other?"

To add to this perceived joyous union of marriage, many French couples choose to work together and raise a family, whereby each member is expected to join the family business when they leave school. I guess this is the backbone of French society, ensuring that each village has at least one *boulangerie*, one butcher's shop, etc., that continues to run when the owners one by one pass on. It is a good system if families can make it work without suffocating each other. The introduction of 'reach for the stars' and 'follow your dreams' would most likely be a fast track to the destruction of French village life.

Clément would often speak to Marc and I about his desire to be free. He had tried many times to split from Laura, but she appeared to be too strong and had no plans to let go. As he returned to his cage for the twentieth time, he muttered to us one day, "What is the point to swap my wife for another woman from France? I go to get only the same woman." I considered his words and thought that it was highly likely that a French woman when considering a trade-in felt the same way about Frenchmen.

From speaking with Mia and learning of her own background and that of Jean-Baptiste, there were few if any good male role models in her family. There also seemed to be a lot of stories that included childhood abandonment. Mia's mother, like the two women who preceded her, had a child with a man who went onto leave her for another woman. In fairness, he did have the finances to live this lifestyle and paid alimony to each of his past mistresses. It was sufficient money for Mia to be sent to a boarding school in Paris. This was a Catholic boarding school and Mia confessed finding it extremely difficult to live within the strict boundaries placed upon her, but she looked to have no choice in the matter. This gave her mother the freedom to find her second man, a married man who was not only extremely well-off and lived in a *château*, but also had a title. Knowing that her husband had a mistress, his wife was not prepared to grant him a divorce as by doing so she would lose her coveted title, so Mia's mother had to be content with being the live-in mistress. It was when Mia went back to see her mother in her new life that she was able to learn about the finer things. Her stepfather spoke to her about antiquities and what to look for and how to sell these for a profit. Living in the *château*, Mia said, was like living in a museum, with oil paintings and a wide array of furniture in each room collected and passed down from the family over several generations. Mia was unsure, when she had finished her education, what to do with her life, but, funded by her stepfather, she was able to travel until she found her first husband. Mia showed me a photo of her husband, a very handsome man who complimented her own beauty. Her marriage unfortunately did not last long when he absconded within a very short time with another lady. She went onto marry her second husband, with whom she conceived Antoine, but he was no better at keeping his peepee in his pants and at one stage she found out he was having an affair simultaneously with both his mistress and the daughter of the mistress. From what Antoine had shared, his father clearly owned a pair of self-removing trousers. He took no interest whatsoever in Antoine, and Mia decided, with very little money and only her beauty to get her by, to swap one side of France for the other in search of a better life.

Jean-Baptiste's story was that his mother became pregnant to a local man around the young age of sixteen. With the embarrassment of this within the family, she was sent away until she had her baby, and her baby boy was then given to her aunt to bring up as her own. His mother went onto meet another man, who gave her five further children before he ended up in jail, something to do with stealing from his employer. This left his mother without any source of income, and she relied upon the kindness of others to feed her children. Jean-Baptiste never had the opportunity to go to school as once he was of working age, around the age of eight, he went out to work in the farms to help towards raising his siblings. When he was twenty-one, he met Mia, a thirty-five-year-old beauty who had only just arrived in his little village. When this young boy clapped eyes on the beautiful Mia, he was keen to have a fling, but Mia, having two failed marriages behind her, anxiously wished to get married and to raise Antoine within a secure family unit. Jean-Baptiste saw an opportunity with this young, well-educated and determined lady to start a business. They had no money between them, but he knew of two ladies within the village who did have some spare money and he talked them into lending it to him. It was by doing so that Mia and Jean-Baptiste were able to start and grow a very successful business.

When Clément came along, they were still working to get their business up and running and decided that the best solution to give them more freedom was to put their boys into boarding school Monday to Friday. It was so sad to hear Mia speak to me about the difficult time Clément experienced at school, and it surprised me after her own poor experience of being placed into a Catholic boarding school at a young age that she was prepared to do the same with her own children. I would listen as she told me stories of a young, anxious and nervous Clément who would regularly be chastised for kicking and punching the teacher. When the boys came home for weekends, these were spent at the shop, and school holidays they were packed off to the opposite end of France where Mia's mother continued to reside.

When Mia used to say, "My boys, Abi, they fight for my attention," I would think, I bet they do, but having got to know these two grown men and the way in which they behaved, I felt sure that the damage had already been done.

It appeared that Laura was keen to distance her own family from that of Clément's. By making this decision, she seemed content with her life, albeit there looked to be a certain amount of surveillance required to keep Clément from finding the keys to his cage. Over one of the four lunches that we all awkwardly shared together, she had confessed that she only ever wanted to be a mother and went onto explain that in France the mother oversees the whole family. "I am the matriarch," she said in a proud tone, similar to the way Mia had communicated her title. The only stories that she shared with us related to her two children who were now partnered up, but that did not stop her from telling them where they could live, what type of house they were to build and what they should and should not be doing. Her children were in their mid and late twenties and yet here she was, sitting proud as punch as she likened herself to a mother hen nurturing her brood. Being a free thinker and raised by parents who sensed when to stop parenting, I could not connect with her thought process. Was 'matriarch' the only title that had been held out to her?

Occasionally, as an ant may choose to leave its leaf, she would leave her small part of the world to accompany Clément to deliver antiquities. Clément was not one for taking trips outside his comfort radius either but together they seemed to find the strength to venture on the occasional day trip to make deliveries. Clément used to speak about clients who lived six hours from his home, and they would both leave at 2am, arriving to take a coffee, make their delivery and proceed to drive all the way home. It didn't appear safe to stay in an unfamiliar part of France.

Clément would complain to us if Laura had spent the day with him in the shop, but he would equally complain if she was at home doing nothing.

"My wife, she do nothing," he would repeatedly say. "She is on the computer all the evening."

We never gave it another thought.

Twelve

Moving house

Marc did not want to be seen as jumping into Ken's shoes when Ken's health took a dramatic turn, and he had quit the Alps to return back to Scotland. It was a small enough community for a lot of background chatter, so Marc had decided to move to another resort to let the dust settle before moving back. Two years later and Marc returned to set up his own business. He was back in his old territory and had the contacts to make this work long-term.

With Beth still at *collège*, we had made the family decision to find another house based in Provence until Beth had finished both *collège* and the *lycée*. We all adored Provence, the flat landscape a refreshing change for Marc after living in the mountains for so many months a year, and we had all gotten used to being together and apart and repeat.

Back in Provence, and just when we thought our relationship with Antoine could not deteriorate any further, when we returned after spending Christmas together in the Alps, our gates opened to what we can only describe as *Steptoe's yard*. I was grateful that Marc was by my side as we entered our garden as I was exhausted battling this ever-descending situation by myself. It seemed that whilst we were away, Antoine had decided to empty out part of the storage unit and had proceeded to scatter the contents from one end of the garden to the other. Gone was our badminton court and as Beth bolted off on a hunt to locate our net, she shouted over that she had finally tracked it down under a stack of old doors. Gone were our parking spaces outside our small terrace. This spreading, of what was none other than decades of stored junk, was unmistakably set out to tell us in no uncertain terms that this was his garden. As Beth carefully observed her surroundings, she chose that moment to tell me of a *Garfield* cartoon she had watched when Jon Arbuckle was at his wits' end and Garfield turned to the camera and said, "Never say that things cannot get any worse. Things can always get worse."

After a reluctant but necessary phone call to Mia, Jean-Baptiste arrived, removed the forklift from the store and proceeded to move the piles of tat over to Antoine's side. He was in an almighty grump but in fairness to him he cleared away enough junk to allow us to park both of our vehicles. I was not going to push my luck by asking him to clear the badminton area.

"Why are there so many problems with your wife and Antoine?" Jean-Baptiste asked Marc as he stopped the forklift and leaned over to speak to us. Marc looked to me for some sort of response, with which I was not forthcoming. "Why do you create problems with him?" he added as he directed his question to me.

There was no real answer to either question, so I treated them both as rhetorical and instead looked into his eyes with what I hoped was a look of despair, shrugged my shoulders and walked off to concentrate on unpacking my car. This was a man who made no secret of how much he despised his stepson. He knew that Antoine was a very jealous person and was coming over too often and yet here he was insinuating that this was my fault. Clément had mentioned to me that his parents thought Antoine had more than friendship in mind for me, and in France in these scenarios,

Clément explained, it is the woman that gets the blame when the man is rejected. I recalled with reluctance *speedo night,* but other than that he had not made any obvious passes in my direction.

To remain in this house now was out of the question. It ceased feeling like home and Antoine was giving his mother such grief, she had ended up suffering a stroke and was rushed into hospital. We found this out when Antoine spotted Marc's van on his next visit and came bounding over clearly in a state of distress and anger.

"Your wife, she is crazy," he said as he used his index finger in a circular motion up to his temple to make what was now becoming the most used sign since our arrival. "My mother, she is in hospital with a stroke because of your wife. Your wife cause so many problems for me and my family."

I chose to watch and listen from my bedroom window, which I had slightly ajar, and wondered how Marc was going to reply to these wild accusations.

I watched as Marc put his hands on Antoine's shoulders and asked him to calm down as until now Antoine had been throwing his arms about as he expressed his anger.

"We are sorry to learn about your mother. Abi loves your mother, you know that well, and I am sure she will go to hospital to visit her as she did the last time." He paused before continuing. "Look at this garden, Antoine. Look at what you have done. Why?"

Antoine followed Marc's finger as Marc pointed out all the items still strewn all over the garden.

"This garden, it is my garden. It is not yours. This house," he said as he pointed at our house, "it is the house of my family. It is not your house. I can do like I want, it is my garden. I can ask who I want to my garden. You…" he continued "…you and your wife have no right to tell me what I can do in my garden."

Marc removed his hands from Antoine's shoulders.

"If you want your garden back, you can have it back, as we are going to look for another house to rent." Marc spoke to Antoine calmly as if he was speaking to a child. "We will soon be gone, and you can have everything back."

As I peered down from my vantage point, I saw Antoine's face starting to relax.

"I think it is better like that. Abi, she was like a sister to me and now she has broken my heart." His sad schoolboy face returned, as did the hand that reached for his heart.

I heard Antoine continue. "You are a good man. It is your wife who is crazy." And with that he toddled off back down the garden and back home.

Marc knew well the craziness of it all, but he also knew that we had probably become too friendly with everyone, letting them into our family life when with hindsight we should have kept them at a distance. I could see and feel Marc's relief as he jumped back into his van and bolted back up to the Alps. Admittedly, I was to blame on reflection for a tiny fraction of it because from Antoine's perspective he just wanted to invite everyone round to share in the good times, good times that he had never thought about creating when he had plenty of opportunity to do so prior to our arrival.

Looking for another rental was not an easy process as we have found that the French are not so trusting with people who are self-employed. They seem to feel more secure when someone has an employer and hence whilst we had tax papers, with Marc setting up a new business, the estate agents asked to see two years' worth of tax documents rather than just the one that I was handing over. Normally, I can talk many a person into many a thing (or so I like to think), but not in this case. The lady was adamant that I was to return in another year and with the correct documents showing our income, she would happily put us forward for a rental. Sigh.

I now had two choices. 1. Speak with Clément to explain our situation and to ask him to keep an ear out for another house, and 2. To type up a letter and to distribute it to all the houses in the neighbouring villages that had a pool. I had no plans to let up with the pool.

Clément had been on this journey with us, somewhat, yet whilst he offered us his personal advice – such as that we should speak to his father and ask him to build a large wall at the back of his brother's house to stop him from entering the garden (what??), I sensed somehow that he was sourcing some pleasure out of our misery. Marc and I had noticed a change in his behaviour when Marc spoke to him about starting a new business and how busy he was in the Alps, where chalet renovation work was booming. It was clear from the look on Clément's face that us succeeding in his country was not going down well. Not well at all. In fact, each time he visited us when Marc returned home, the first question he would ask was "How much you win now in the Alps?" The French use the word *gagner* that can translate into *to win* or *to earn*, so Clément would elect to translate the term into *to win* when addressing the subject of earning money.

Marc always played things down and would respond that whilst he was doing well, it was doubtful that he was doing as well as Clément and this, we could see, rocked his boat as we moved the subject quickly away from money.

Over Christmas, Clément had also gifted Antoine a puppy, a puppy that was conceived seemingly when his dog had gone walkabout. We now had an abandoned puppy in the garden, one that was sent out to poop and one that waited at the gates for any opportunity to do a runner. This meant that when we were entering or leaving the garden in our car, Beth had to watch for the dog as it only took a mini second for this dog to smell freedom and make a run for it. (Who could blame her?) Often, when we caught up with her, she would bite because she had not been trained to do otherwise. She was in desperate need of love and attention as she had a good nature as opposed to Thomas' dog, but it was getting neither, albeit that Beth and I, when we looked out and saw her sitting dejected by the gates, would often run out with a tennis ball so we could play catch with her. I questioned Antoine's desire to own a dog when he already had a cat and an ex-wife living with him and was showing no interest whatsoever in spending time with his new acquisition.

I broached the subject of moving house one afternoon with Clément when he texted me to ask what I was up to. I explained that I had in fact distributed letters that morning to the nearby villages to see if anyone was interested in a private let. I expected a response something along the lines of, *That seems like a good idea*, or something similar, but instead I was quite taken aback at his clearly incensed reply.

Abi, I ask my father to give you this house with no tax papers and now if you go to leave this is bad for me and I go to be in bad relation with my father. Why you want to move? You must stay. It is not good for me if you leave and my parents go not to be happy. If they are not happy, they make me not happy. You must sort this out with my brother. My brother, he is crazy. I am in bad relation with him. I go not to be happy if you move.

This was the first of many texts that afternoon, unwelcomed communication that felt controlling and manipulative. It wasn't threatening but it was seeing things only from his perspective and not from ours. Finally, that evening, as he continued to rant by text, I had no option but to put him on block.

Clément owned a few rental houses, forming part of his boasting material when he sat like a peacock crowing on about his alleged wealth. The house that he owned, that I had my eye on, was situated in a quaint village, one that we visited frequently as it was a village that hosted many fêtes throughout the year. I would remark to Beth at times that it was a village that could use any excuse to hold a fête, i.e., 'granny hanging out her old knickers' could have been such an excuse as each fête was very similar to the other; the same stalls setting out locally produced saucisson, preserves, honey, various types of cheese, fresh pasta, various crafts, wine and beer and the half baguette filled with a sausage for a snack. With live music at various intervals throughout the day, it was a pleasant way to pass the time, nursing a plastic cup of local wine or beer and bumping into locals for a brief chat about the weather. Beth loved the stall that sold goat's cheese. In particular, the cheese that was formed into the shape of a heart; soft, creamy, tangy and delicious, especially when matched with a rustic baguette and a glass of local wine. One of life's simple pleasures. The any-excuse approach to holding a fête was the idea of the *mairie,* anxious to support the local shops and producers throughout the year. A rocking idea.

Back to the house that I had my eye on, and when I had mentioned it to Marc, he reminded me that the house had been rented out for the past ten years so it was doubtful that it would come up for rent anytime soon. Neither Marc nor I wanted to rent another house from this family, and we hoped that maybe something else would come up from my letter writing, but I was realistic and knew that it was likely to come down to Clément or stay where we were.

Three months later and Beth and I were in the Alps with Marc, when Marc received a phone call from Clément. His tenants had just given him notice and were planning to move out within the next few months; did we want to move in? According to Clément, his tenant was in the process of buying her own house and was just waiting to sign the paperwork.

Upon our return to Provence, Beth and I arranged to visit the house with Clément. A three-bedroom house, with three separate terraces and its own pool. Beth and I were happy. A quick phone call to Marc and he was happy that we were happy, and we struck a deal with Clément. It was the same rent as we had paid to his father and one month's deposit.

Towards the end of June that year, we were all packed up. We had left our house in a far better condition than we had found it in. The house was freshly painted, we left a woodburning stove in the fireplace to replace the unpractical open fire, and blinds on the windows. We had also transformed the front terrace with clay tiles that Clément had donated and a fence that finally gave this small area complete privacy. As Jean-Baptiste walked around, he offered Marc money for the wood burning stove but, in truth, Marc had been given this from a client in the Alps who had no use for it, and with it being so heavy, we did not want to go carting it about. We had heard also that it was very difficult to receive a deposit back in France and so we hoped that this would make the process easy. An envelope was handed over to Marc at the end of the tour with the full amount returned, and Marc kicked himself for not asking for money for the stove.

Like the last house, our new place was perched by a road, but this road was far quieter than the last one. On this occasion, you had to climb up stairs to reach the house, which meant that the garden and pool were away from the road, plus there was the bonus of having large trees and bushes surrounding the garden, cutting down the noise and giving our newfound space complete privacy. The pool was small compared to our last one, but it was adequate, and beside the pool there sat a pool house and across from the pool house an expanse of lawn large enough to set up our badminton court. A gate led to the back of the house, to a BBQ area and large terrace, and from there down to the side of the house, which had a tiled terrace with a doorway that led into the kitchen. It was a compact house of around 100 m2 with three double bedrooms, an open living/dining room, kitchen and bathroom. The house also came with a garage, with a secondary garage attached being retained by the family.

Laura and Clément had asked Marc and I to meet them at the house on the evening before we were to move in. As we parked and walked up the stairs towards the house, I felt a strange mix of feelings ranging from relief to impending doom.

The door was open, so we shouted our greetings as we walked into the hallway and into the living room to find Clément and Laura rubbing their hands against the wall as they appeared to be looking for some sort of damage, or maybe dampness. Clément looked to be making his conclusions as Laura noted them down. The French are notorious for renting out a house and expecting it to be in the same condition as when they handed it over. *Wear* and *tear* are not two words the French are supposedly familiar with.

The usual *bisous* over with, Clément was quick to get down to business.

"I give you the house for not much money," he said (although it was the same amount as what we had paid to his father). "All I ask is that you renovate it and make it better, like you did for my father."

Marc and I glanced at each other and back to Clément as this was the first mention of renovating their house.

"We will keep the house good," Marc replied. "Show me this that you wish me to repair, and I will do it."

With that, they took Marc to the outside laundry room and asked for him to replace the back door. That seemed easy enough. As they proceeded to walk us around the house, they kindly offered that if we wished to pull out the old kitchen and install a new one or indeed renovate the bathrooms or install walk-in wardrobes, we were free to do so! There was no hiding the fact that they thought we were both stupid. The French, it turns out, do not leave anything behind in their rentals, seldom paint them and certainly do not improve them prior to handing them back.

There was no paperwork to sign, no detailed inventory to indicate how outmoded the house was and no mention of the cracks on the walls caused by subsidence or the state of the shutters and the antiquated bathrooms. They had our deposit, and as we walked around, I kept a close eye on these two. Clément was behaving nervously and was occasionally glancing up to Laura in a knowing fashion. Laura was her usual curt self, desperate to wrap this all up and leave. They were either up to something or I was developing paranoia. Time would tell.

A word commonly used here in France is *arnaque*, which translates into English as scam or rip-off. Others can interpret such scams as games. Due to their polite manner, the French can carry off *arnaques* very well, and this means that you must always be on your guard.

As I watched these two trade glances at each other, I recalled conversations that we had shared over lunch with Laura during which she would throw her head back and laugh, when relating a story about something unfortunate that had happened to someone. It was almost like a witch's cackle and yet here I was about to take keys from this woman. Just prior to them leaving, she dug into her large handbag and pulled out an instruction manual for the pool robot. "This is a very expensive robot," she explained in French in a very condescending manner. "It is still under guarantee if you should have any problems with it." With that, she said her goodbyes and just about dashed down the stairs. I was familiar with the robot; it was the same one that fell apart at Antoine's and one that had ceased being manufactured several years ago due to it being a shit robot. I knew from Clément that he had bought the same robot as Antoine and had told us that his had broken down too and confirmed that it was indeed 'sheet'. Had they found someone to make a temporary repair so it could be passed onto us with the sole intention of it breaking down and us having to replace it to the original value? The answer undoubtedly was yes. We were being taken for fools.

As we returned to our house to pack up the rest of our belongings, we realised with sadness that there were going to be no goodbyes to this side of the family. Clément had informed me that my friendship with his mother had been questioned by Antoine as he felt sure that my relationship with his mother was solely down to me looking for an inheritance. According to Clément, Mia was also starting to suspect my intentions (not that I could believe everything uttered by Clément as he liked to sow doubt). I thought back to all the lunches by the pool, the countless hospital visits when Mia had suffered her first stroke and found herself in hospital for several months. Despite Antoine receiving a large sum of money prior to his mother's stroke, he chose not to visit her in hospital. His reason? He didn't like hospitals. I thought back to the laughs we all shared when I visited her each month to pay our rent or just to call in to have a chat. Mia calling round to see Antoine late in the afternoon would often result in her coming over to see me as we sat out on the terrace or beside the pool enjoying a little tipple of something. I chose to believe that Mia and I had become friends, but I could see that with recent events her attitude towards me had changed, and despite her asking for me to continue to call in, I sensed that our friendship had reached a conclusion. It made sense to cut ties.

Life had become tough for Mia. She rarely left her house; such was the palaver of having to do so. When we first met her, she could walk to my house from Antoine's but as the years progressed and she suffered her first stroke, she found it easier to get about in her wheelchair. She had recently installed a chair lift in her home, but even taking that into consideration, left to her husband, it wasn't easy for them both to leave the house. It was often just too much effort. This would mean that Mia would spend her days phoning her family and discussing every minute detail of what was happening in their lives and in the lives of everyone they knew. Rarely did anything major happen so it was generally left to gossip and general tittle-tattle. The old saying that if someone is gossiping about others to you, they are most likely doing the same behind your back rang true. Mia was a good lady; she had a good heart. She was exhausted by the fluctuating relationships she had with her children and with her grandchildren. In all the years we had gotten to know this family, never was there a time when they could be classed as one big happy family.

"I am in bad relations with my father" was a common statement by Clément.

"I am in bad relations with my grandfather" was a common statement if we ever bumped into Clément's son and asked about the welfare of his family.

"My husband is in bad relations with Clément. It is sending me mad" was a common statement from Mia.

"I am in bad relations with my granddaughter. She comes to see me only when she wants money" was another common complaint from Mia.

Over four years of "My brother, he is crazy" from both Clément and Antoine.

And their lives, whether we were part of them or not, were likely to continue in the same manner until one by one they left this earth to gain peace somewhere else.

The morning after we had moved in, we made the decision to dig deep and put all doubts away. We reasoned that we had lived amongst the suspicious French for a fair amount of time, and it was likely that we had unwittingly picked up upon their mistrust of others. So, that morning, I flung open our shutters with renewed zeal, donned my bikini, put the coffee machine on and, attempting not to have a care in the world, meandered out to the front garden for my morning swim.

I returned to the house to find a text from Clément that read in French: *Why you only give me one month's deposit for the house? I asked you for two.*

He had only ever asked me for one. The game had commenced.

Thirteen

Something afoot

Our fifth long hot summer wasn't dissimilar to our first when we had the garden and pool to ourselves, at least initially, and were able to enjoy each other's company without strangers descending upon us. Guests were of course allowed but by invitation only. My father and his wife, her son, daughter-in-law and granddaughter had arrived for a two-week vacation and had rented a beautiful house in one of the neighbouring villages.

As they were flying economy on the final flight of the day, it made sense for me to collect the keys to the house and thereafter meet my family at the airport to guide them back to their holiday accommodation. It was likely their flight would be late.

We finally arrived at the house, which was situated high on a mountaintop village with few road signs, to the point where even the lady in the satnav was starting to lose the plot. There was a considerable deposit for the house and my family were keen for me to ensure that all was in order prior to their arrival. All appeared to be well organized as I read through a list of instructions that came with the house to work the air conditioning, and strict instructions not to pour bleach down the drains, etc. It all seemed reasonable, and they looked to have covered everything. The garden housed a beautiful swimming pool with a large outdoor kitchen installed into a renovated pool house. I knew my family would love this house the moment they clapped eyes upon it.

A couple of days had passed and one morning, as I was taking them up some fresh croissants for breakfast, I noticed that a green line had appeared around the rim of the pool.

"What is that?" I asked my stepbrother as I pointed over to the line.

"I know, we were wondering the same thing as the green is also under the inflatables. Do you think there is a problem with the chemicals in the pool?" he asked.

I knew for sure that that was no green line when I visited the house to collect the keys, and I had never experienced this in my own pool, which was also fibreglass. Was it the sun cream? I wondered. I had always found that when my family came over, they were always applying sun cream because, of course, their skin was unaccustomed to sunshine, whereas Beth and I rarely ever used it and opted to cover up when we felt we'd had enough sun. This meant that when my family left, there was always a greasy residue left on the surface of the water, but it had never left a mark.

"I think we should try to remove it," I suggested, "and if we cannot do so, I will call the owner and ask her to send the pool guys over to check the chemicals."

Scrubbing brush in hand, my stepbrother got to work, but try as he might, the green line did not budge. I notified the owner, and she sent in the pool company.

"You must have put something in the pool," they said as they also looked puzzlingly at the green line.

"We haven't put anything in the pool," my stepbrother confirmed.

We had checked the instruction sheet again that came with the house and we did not see anything about the avoidance of sun cream in the pool.

We were all at a loss as to what had caused the green line, which looked to have been absorbed into the fibreglass. No amount of scrubbing or bicarbonate of soda or *Cif* was making any difference.

It was a spoiler to their holiday, and it was only after their holiday had finished that we finally came up with a possible reaction between the sun cream and copper. My family had been using normal sun cream for themselves but had chosen to use a high factor one for their young daughter. The high factor cream looked to have reacted with the copper in the water, copper that was an ingredient of the solution added each winter to stop the pool from forming algae. We had never used any solution in our pool previously because at the end of the winter we simply emptied the pool because we had our own underground spring; however, due to the cost of replacing the water each year, added to that the possible damage that can occur when the fibreglass pool is empty, people tend to keep the same water year after year and just add chemicals, thus creating a buildup of copper.

It was a very unfortunate incident, and no one was truly at fault but after their stay, the owner's pool was damaged and I found myself caught up in a very heated debate. The final solution was that the owner would keep half the deposit and put it towards a pool freeze to cover up the line. My family were annoyed, but it seemed to be the only valid solution. On the plus side, I now had a fibreglass pool and I doubted that it had been emptied and thankfully my family had not used it on their visit, or I would undoubtedly have had the same problem, and I doubted that the option of a freeze would have been swallowed by either Clément or Laura.

At our new house, our neighbours, of whom there were many, were calling over to introduce themselves one by one. They all seemed friendly, but I was keen to share with them as little information as I could get away with. Friendly = nosy = gossip.

One of our neighbours seemed a little put out that we had moved in and was brazen enough to directly ask me how we were able to rent the house. I explained that we had known the family for several years and had rented from his father in another village, and when this house became available, we were first to be offered it. My new neighbour made no effort to hide his displeasure with my response and I wondered whether he had had his eye on renting it.

"You must be careful. This house has been robbed many times. They enter through the back window. When you go on holiday, it is important that you let us know and we will watch the house for you," he informed me in French. He appeared somewhat genuine, but I could not be sure. My grandfather always told us children that if you wanted your house to be robbed, you told your local bobby you were going on holiday. I was going to stick with that advice.

Another of our neighbours had phoned Clément, who of course was now our new proprietor, not long after we had moved in to complain that the garage door was making a rattling sound when cars drove by and could he speak to us about repairing it? In all fairness, she had tried to speak to Marc about it but as she pointed at the garage and rambled away quickly in French, Marc had not a clue what she was saying and came back up to tell me that as far as he could make out, our neighbour wanted to rent our garage.

"I had your neighbour phone me and I am not happy of that. You must get Marc to fix the garage. I do not want another phone call with a complaint," were Clément's sharp remarks when he called me into his shop to inform me of the phone call he had received from his old neighbour. He must have known that the garage door had made a shuddering sound as he had lived in the house previously for eighteen years, and yet nothing had been mentioned to us until we received the complaint. I had heard the slight rattle of the garage doors but in truth I did not think anything of it.

"Are my neighbours crazy?" I asked him as I made the usual and familiar sign for crazy.

"*Oui*," he replied, "you must go to be careful."

Sigh.

The couple that had phoned in their complaint were an older couple, maybe in their mid-sixties. He was tallish and thin, retired, and spent his early mornings hunting when it was the season to do so, which always seemed to be the season to do so. If he wasn't hunting, he was gardening or clearing out his garage. He seemed neither a seducer nor a predator, although with his camouflage gear on most days, he was certainly out hunting something. His wife was small and plump and appeared still to be working as she sped off each morning and returned home around 6pm with her car windows down and classical music blasting out.

I made sure to *bonjour* my neighbours and discuss the weather when I saw them, and left it at that.

As we wound our way down the year towards Christmas, I discovered that I had a doorbell and ran down to the gate to find my small plump neighbour waiting for me. What is it now? I thought as I ran through what possible noises I could be making. I needn't have worried as there she was holding a bag that contained sweets and a few small battery operated tealights as a gift for Beth and I. It was such a lovely and welcoming touch, and I quickly forgave her in my mind for her initial complaint to Clément. The French mindset in these parts was possibly, think the worst until proven otherwise.

Christmas was spent in our new place. We had purchased a fire pit for the back terrace and Marc had inherited a Mexican stove from one of his clients as well as an outdoor settee, which made the pool house a welcoming option when the weather was inclement.

The winter went by quickly with the usual comings and goings back and fore to the Alps. As had become the custom, Marc would call in to see Clement when he returned home and they would visit a restaurant to have a catch up.

As they both chatted over lunch, Clement enquired as to the price of the 4WD Marc had recently purchased. Marc wasn't keen to delve into such details and related that he had bought it at a reasonable price from Ken who had returned to Scotland. Marc diverted the conversation towards the house and how happy we were living in it and thanked him for giving us the opportunity to rent it. As Marc was about to drop Clement back at his shop, Clement casually mentioned that he had recently been offered a million euros by a developer to buy our house so the land could be turned into apartments. He claimed to be considering the offer.

"If I was you, Clément, I would take it," said Marc, feeling that this was an invented story designed to unsettle us. "No one is going to offer you anymore. You should take it."

We had become accustomed to Clément inventing stories that were designed to inflate his ego.

"I think I go to say no to him," replied Clément.

There was no more mention of the developer after that day, but I was under no illusion that he had given us the house out of kindness. We realized also that with Clement being our new proprietor it may prove awkward for us all to remain friends. He had stopped calling in for a beer unless he specifically wished for Marc to do some work for him at his shop. He did however continue to text us both frequently eager to know where we each were, what we were doing and how much money we were 'winning'. There was a vindictive side that reared its ugly head now and again with put-down comments that made me wonder if he was intentionally out to create problems for us.

The following year at the start of summer, I was surprised to receive a text from Clement asking for me to visit his shop as he wished to speak to me about something. I wondered what it could be and hoped it wasn't another complaint by any of our neighbours as, to be honest, we had been a bit noisy recently, with Beth and I having a pretend Glastonbury night on a night where there was a terrific storm. The lightning and thunder were rocking our little village and the rain was heaving it down, so we decided to make the most of the weather noise and turned our music up full blast, got out two brooms and sang the night away. Our pool house made a fantastic stage, and our imaginary crowd was going crazy for us and kept asking for encores, taking our show later into the evening than we had expected. Had anyone heard our racket? It was hard to say, but we doubted it.

As I walked into Clément's shop, I found him sitting on a dining chair, which was part of a dining set that he had on display. He looked rather sombre, but he was the kind of man who was either 'I am the king of the castle' or 'I am a lion in a cage', so it wasn't always straight forward predicting what mood he was in. After the usual *bisous* and pleasantries, he announced:

"Abi, I am no longer your proprietor. Laura and I, we go for divorce. I keep my house and Laura, she take your house and the one next door, which we own too. She go to move next door to you. She go to be your new neighbour." He was avoiding eye contact when he was dishing out his news, which meant only one thing: he was up to something.

"If you need anything, you must ask my wife. Your house is not to do with me." Clement had never learned the art of telling lies, his facial expression gave him away every time. Something was going on. I could smell it, as Clément himself might be heard to say.

I was not surprised at the split, knowing their track record, but I was a little shocked that she was planning to move next door to me. I now knew Laura well enough to know that she disliked most females as well as foreigners, and in particular, those who were not fluent in French. Falling into all these categories, we were never likely to be friends, especially when I considered that on each occasion when we all ate together, Clément went out of his way to compliment me on what I was wearing or how I was looking, with the likely intention of furthering his wife's jealousy, especially towards me. This was a compliment card that he played with too much effort for it to be taken seriously by me, and it only took a glance at Laura, who would sit with her glasses perched at the end of her nose, for me to see her angry reaction. She may have remained silent when he played the joking, flirtatious Frenchman but her eyes were fierce, and I felt them burn into my soul.

"I am sorry to hear that you and your wife have problems," I said, concluding quickly from his strange behaviour that he was looking for a negative reaction from his news, and I wanted to give him the opposite of that which he craved. "I am happy to have Laura live next to me and if I need anything I will knock her door. In fact," I added, "I think I go to ask her to play tennis with me."

As a child, *Little Miss Contrary* by Roger Hargreaves was my favourite character. I had learnt at a young age that sometimes it was more beneficial, as well as amusing, to give the opposite reaction to that which was predicted.

With that, I thanked Clément for letting me know the change of proprietor and casually walked out to the car, waving my goodbyes.

Sure enough, a few weeks after speaking with Clément, I watched as my neighbour moved out and Laura moved in. Clement had mentioned to Marc that the house that they lived in was his house because the land he had built it on was an early inheritance from his father. It seemed they had chosen the marriage contract, *le régime de la séparation de biens*. A contract that allows for two people to live together whilst keeping their finances separately. Laura was therefore claiming back their old house which she had purchased from her uncle and the one next door, which they had built later on, and the one to which she was now moving into.

It wasn't long after she had moved next door that one by one my neighbours came over to speak to me about her attitude. This was a road whereby many of the houses were built long before cars had been invented, so whilst there were a lot of houses, not helped by many of them being divided up into apartments, there were very few spaces available for homeowners to park their cars. The house that Laura was staying in rested at the bottom of our garden and had a small driveway and a parking space directly outside. When turning out of her house to the right-hand side, there were around six parking spaces under the shade of the trees that protected our garden and led down to our house. We had three parking spaces outside our house, so we had no need to park there, but for our neighbours this area was esssential. One of our neighbours made the error of parking directly outside her house when he had returned home late one evening and there was nowhere else to park. Seemingly, she left an angry note on his car and apparently, according to my neighbour, damaged his car intentionally. He was warned that if he parked outside her house again, she would stop everyone from parking in the area between her house and ours as she now owned all the land. This did not go down well with my neighbours, but she was my proprietor and lived at the bottom of my garden so what was I supposed to say?

Up until now, I was thankful not to have spoken to Laura and several weeks had gone by.

In the middle of July, with my sister and her husband having arrived for their summer holidays, we had spent one afternoon drinking champagne by the pool when I heard the doorbell chime. I quickly threw on my linen shirt over my bikini before running down to see who it was.

There in front of me, with her washed-out and bobbly tee-shirt teamed up with her denims preserved from the 80s, stood Laura.

"I do not know if Clément has told you that I am your new proprietor," she said in French, handing her bank details over to me as I opened the gate to let her into the garden.

"Yes," I replied. "Clément has told Marc and me," and then as we both reached the top of the stairs and up into the garden, I added in French, "you must be happy now to be free?" In truth, I do not know where these words came from. I suppose after seeing her and Clément together and the fact that this was separation number twenty-one, in my tipsy state I must have concluded that there had to be an element of happiness now she was living on her own. The words sort of fell out of my mouth and I regretted having said them immediately, but to add to the ridiculousness of the question that I had just posed, I threw my arms into the air to indicate the feeling of freedom.

As I waited for her response, she just stood there staring at me in the manner, I suppose, in which a sober person regards someone who has spent the afternoon drinking champagne, and replied simply, "*Oui.*"

I was nervous. I did not trust this female who was standing in my garden. She had a bad reputation and did not display any sign of friendliness, so as she just stood there, I kept nervously chatting. "I love to be free," I announced, to which I recall waving my arms about again as if to accentuate the point.

She just stood there looking at me weirdly, so my sister held out her arm to offer her a chair to sit and have a glass of champagne with us. Thankfully she shook her head to decline our invitation and headed back down the stairs and back to her house at the bottom of my garden. *Merci dieu,* as that afternoon was likely to have sunk lower than it already had as, unbeknown to me, I had just asked my new proprietor if she was going to enjoy putting herself about, because I certainly loved to. *Libre* in French does not refer to freedom of spirit, such as the way I had translated it, but instead freedom of the use of what is tucked away in your pants. Shit!

It wasn't a great start, and I was not to realise my mistake until a long time after that. I found it difficult at times to get it into my thick skull that the French were not an excitable nation. The use of the word *excitement* also had sexual connotations. What was wrong with the French?

Whilst having her own two car park spots, Laura decided one week to park her car outside my house. What she was driving is also part of the story.

Laura was the proud owner of a black Audi A5. This eventuated after a conversation with Clément when he made a surprise visit to have a beer with Marc and me one afternoon a few weeks before their latest separation.

"I do not care for the car," announced Clément. "I do not understand why people must have a Mercedes, BMW or an Audi. A car is a car, it is nothing."

I thought back to the games we used to play with Antoine when we left things out to see if he would buy a better version, and a thought sprang to mind.

"I love my Audi A3," I announced. "I would have preferred an Audi A5, but I will have to wait as it is too expensive for us at the moment."

It didn't take long, maybe two weeks maximum, and I received a text from Clément to tell me that he had bought Laura a new car. A picture followed of Laura sitting behind the wheel of a black Audi A5. He had added to his text that he had purchased the top-of-the-range version, and did I want to come to see it? Nope.

Outside my house therefore sat Laura's black Audi A5.

It was rather annoying, especially when she had two car park spaces outside her own house, so it was there for a reason. These two were consumed by jealousy and I presume they thought other people were the same. In truth, I have never understood jealousy because I have always believed in working hard to achieve what I wanted in my life and having my own set of goals rather than living the life of others, which made it so much harder to understand what I was now dealing with.

Several weeks later, the Audi had disappeared and, in its place, parked outside her house sat her old Peugeot. Where was her Audi?

Clément was quick to inform us that their relationship had broken down further and that they had met with a lawyer to discuss getting a divorce. Clément was not looking for a divorce, he said; he wished only to be free for a while as he was set on joining up with some *libertines* who were meeting women they had found on Facebook. From what I had gathered over the years of them splitting, it was always Clément who initiated it and Clément again who decided when she was to come back home. This was the first time I was aware of that she had moved into another house as normally she just went back to her parents' house until Clément realised he was unable to manage on his own and grovelled his way back into her good books, this information previously being gathered from Mia and Antoine, of course.

One hot afternoon as I was sitting having a glass of wine with Marc in the coolness of the pool house, we discussed the oddness of our situation that within six months of me mentioning to Clément that we were looking for another house, his tenants were out, and we were in. When Laura and Clément split up, the tenant next to us had left, and she had moved in. It was then that it dawned on us. They had no hesitation in asking their tenants to move out when it suited them. Whilst on the one hand it had initially worked in our favour, we could also see that they played the role of proprietors by their own rules. We knew that we had to put plans in place to move to the Alps, sooner rather than later.

When Marc had called in to catch up with Clément, he learnt that Laura did not have sufficient money to make the repayments for the Audi, so he took it off her and gave her back her old Peugeot. The Audi was now parked outside his shop.

Interestingly, she never once parked her old Peugeot outside our house.

I was worried that summer that Laura would complain about noise, as Beth and I were apt to watch movies outside and we loved musicals, which generally meant a lot of singing. We also enjoyed dancing late into the evening, particularly when my sisters came to visit. To be fair to Laura, she never once complained but that did not stop me from imagining her doing so, and that summer, it is fair to say, I was on edge. To all intents and purposes, however, if Clément ever asked, I always told him that everything was good and what a great summer we were having.

September had arrived, the time of year when the pool temperature drops to the point where swimming ceases to be a pleasurable experience, and as I forced myself into the pool for the final time that year, I could smell not just emissions of the usual one chimney coming from the bottom of my garden but those of two. It could only mean one thing, and a quick look to the front of the house to see Clément's Audi confirmed that a reunion was on the cards.

My wife, he chose to share by text, *she says, Clément, I do not come back to you this easy. You must work more hard to be a better husband. She want half of everything I have worked for, so I go back to be with her again. I love my wife. I go back.*

It was a relief when I saw Clément's van pull up and empty out their house, a house over the course of the summer she had spent 8,000€ on furnishing. Clément had mentioned that after he turned her out/asked her to leave/she voluntarily left (who the hell knows), the first thing he did was to replace his bed and have the house repainted. He was not a happy man when he pulled out the fridge in preparation for the arrival of the decorator and noticed that the back of it was dirty. "My wife, she does not do a good job to clean my house," was a complaint he had made to Marc. Now four months later and they were back together.

If I was a betting girl and there was an option to bet on what was going to happen next, I could have made a fortune, because I was learning to predict this French Bulldog with behavioural issues.

Clément proclaimed to both Marc and me that he was overjoyed with his reunion with his wife. They had agreed that she could return to stay in his house whilst retaining her rentals to allow her to continue to be our proprietor. It was playing out as predicted thus far.

Beth and I had been up to see Marc a few times. It was not so easy now because he was staying in a one-bedroom apartment so for us all to be together, it meant planning ahead and renting something bigger. His business was growing rapidly, to the point that we had spotted and purchased our own renovation project: an old mountain house set over three floors. Other than its four solid walls, it needed a replacement everything, but it was an opportunity too good to miss.

It was on the drive back down south that I experienced an unusual sinking feeling. I recalled locking up the house and bolting the shutters, but I couldn't help but feel that we were returning to a house that had been burgled. It was the first time that I had felt this way since my neighbourly warning, considering all the journeys back and forth that we had made.

As I opened my front door, I could feel a cold draft coming down the long corridor and as I approached my bedroom, I could see that the shutters had been forced and my bedroom window remained open. There was no glass broken as they knew how to kick open an old-style window. My dressing table sat by the window, and I could see that the contents of the jewellery drawer had been carefully raked through and a gold necklace was missing as well as a long necklace that, whilst it had no monetary value, was one that I had become attached to. Drawers had been pulled out of both bedside cabinets as well as our large pine chest of drawers. Marc had a stash of money under one of the cabinets which, despite being a stash, was French francs, 20,000 of them, tucked into an envelope that fell out of a ceiling of a property that Marc had been renovating. Marc was very attached to his stash despite their lack of value and was relieved to learn that they remained where he had hidden them. Fortunately, the rest of the house had not been touched other than a small amount of money being taken from Beth's purse, which she had left beside her bed.

I called Clément as I did not have Laura's number, and he put me on loudspeaker so I could speak to her. Neither of them seemed interested in what had happened other than to ask if there was any damage to their property, which of course there was. Learning this, they suggested that Marc come home to repair it that evening. It was now around 10pm, so this was out of the question, and I insisted that with them being landlords, they send someone over to do the repairs. With that, they relented and agreed to send over their son Michael.

We had gotten to know Michael over the years, a boy in his mid-twenties who was very much controlled by his parents, so on this occasion he had no option but to follow their instructions. I always found him to be friendly but this evening when he arrived, and we sat in the kitchen having a coffee, he asked me if the robbers had taken anything, to which I replied, yes, two necklaces and some money out of Beth's purse. His next question took me by surprise.

"Did they take Marc's money?"

What money? I should have replied but instead I said no, they had not taken anything else. What made them believe that Marc had cash in the house? Why were they keen to know if it had been taken? Suddenly I started to suspect Clément.

Michael said it was necessary to call the police, which he did on my behalf, and within fifteen minutes I had two policemen in my bedroom dusting my window and dressing table, looking for fingerprints. It had been a cold evening and I thought surely the burglars were not so stupid as to break in without gloves, if even just to keep their hands warm. It was like a scene set in the 1950s as they searched for prints.

I recalled a year or so previous when Clément and Laura were burgled as they were out enjoying a meal. The burglars had supposedly taken 15,000€, cash, which Clément had squirreled away but had failed to hide in a secure location. I remember a day or so after the event Clément calling in to see us and referring to the experience as 'like he had been raped'. Was it though? Could or should a robbery be likened to rape? I thought.

The odd thing about the break-in was that ever since our neighbour had informed us that we were going to be robbed and how they were going to access our house, Beth and I had been prepared for this to happen, waiting, in fact. Whilst we secured the house with all the bolts and bars put in place to secure the shutters, Michael had explained that it was easy to break into a French house and explained how kicking the middle part of the window released the lock, allowing them to enter quickly and easily. Getting through the shutter was just a case of using an axe and breaking the top panel to reach down to unbolt from the inside.

Beth confessed to me that evening that she was glad it was over with, as she had worried about her house being burgled each time we had left to see Marc. Now she felt relieved that it had finally happened. Strangely, we both felt the same, but nonetheless we installed a burglar alarm.

There was also the *Famous Five* mystery of the disappearing mail. Parcels were going missing and yet there were few people who ever walked past our house, other than neighbours who had parked their cars, so who was stealing our mail? Was it our neighbours, as other than that how did anyone know that parcels were being delivered unless they had access to my phone, a thought, in truth, I had not considered.

Christmas that year came and went quickly, as always, and February was spent with part of my UK family who had their own chalet in the French Alps and had come over to ski. As we all sat enjoying our lunch in the winter sunshine, we started to speak about a virus that was starting to spread in these parts. Marc had in fact come home during January feeling quite unwell and had spent several days in bed, which was not like him at all. His friend too was ill, far worse than Marc, and was in bed for over a week. We had put it down to the usual winter flu and as Beth and I were unaffected, we never gave it another thought, but as we holidayed that February it was something that everyone was talking about. The virus in the Alps was spreading like wildfire.

As coronavirus/COVID took hold, like everyone else, we were put on lockdown when we returned to Provence. As all three of us sat having lunch in the spring sunshine, we reasoned that it wasn't going to make a great deal of difference to our lives as Marc's industry was given permission to continue to work and, with this news, he made his mind up to return to the Alps as soon as possible. Beth was going to find herself, like every other child, being educated from her laptop and other than that, life was going to continue for us in a similar manner as before, albeit no trips to the beach and no eating out. We were each extraordinarily grateful for where we had chosen to be located during this time as summer approached.

Neither Marc nor I had heard anything from Clément during lockdown and after several weeks had passed, we each opted to send him a text to ensure that all was okay with him and his family. He had replied to say that Laura and himself had been staying at her parents' farm throughout the duration of lockdown and this aspect itself was making him crazy, as Laura was keeping a close eye on his every movement and he was desperate to regain some freedom. There was also the great unknown about when he would be able to return to work as his bills continued to mount.

A week or so later, I received a panicked and unexpected text from Clément, something along the lines of having sent some antiques overseas and having lost touch with his client, who had yet to pay. To lighten the darkness of his mood, I replied, *Stay positive. I am sure he will pay you.* And I added, *Things go to return one day as before, and you will soon be back in your shop chatting up all your ladies again.*

I could sense he was not in a mood to be humoured and to my astonishment, I received the following text. It read, *Abi, I am a predator. My wife, she checks my messages, and she is a very jealous woman.* As much as I chose to laugh about his typically French behaviour towards women, I was taken aback when he chose to use the word *predator* to refer to himself. Was I being too serious, I wondered, or was this a warning? If he was going to ask us to leave, lockdown was as good a time as ever and would cause us the most inconvenience. I was on standby.

Several weeks had passed since receiving what was to be the last text I would ever receive from Clément, and as I sat on the pavers happily repotting some garden plants, I heard a text come in. As I reached up to the table to collect my phone, I saw that it was from an unfamiliar number. It read in French, *I have found a text from you on my husband's phone. He is MY husband, and you live in MY house. I give you six months to get out. Laura*

The Rottweiler had been released.

I replied immediately that yes, I had contacted her husband to ensure that all was okay with him, as had Marc, and that there was nothing for her to be worried about. I assured her that I did not have eyes for her husband and did she want to call around for a coffee to discuss? It was going to have to be a distant coffee, but I thought it still best to offer.

She simply replied with the words, *Six months.*

Marc was busy and I did not wish to bother him with what amounted to no more than nonsense. Marc was aware that Clément would text me occasionally and had warned me that if his wife found out there would be trouble, but how was I supposed to stop him? Clément to me was a comedy French predator, a man with low self-esteem that played any game where the result allowed him to feel strong and dominant. I was strong enough to call him up and point out his flaws and in truth this was giving me the strength to deal with similar men that roamed in these parts. Marc and I had a lot on our minds when we arrived in France, and a Frenchman calling in for a beer and venting his thoughts on women was unexpected and, to be honest, much of what he said went over our heads initially because he was thinking in French and us in British. As he prattled on with his brain stuck in the Dark Ages, Marc and I had more serious things on our minds, such as how we were going to make money and buy a house. His remarks we viewed simply as trivial and most likely typically French, and whilst I can still recall some of his comments, which were designed for that purpose, I guess, for the most part we dismissed them.

When I mentioned to Mia the poor behaviour I was experiencing from some Frenchmen, she agreed that she too had found them to be difficult and it was worse being married to one.

"My husband," she said, "he may appear happy and jolly to you but when the door is closed, he is nothing like that and he is a difficult man to be with." She paused before continuing. "Would it help," she asked, "if I taught you to become more Provençal in your ways?" Eh? No, thanks!

So, that crazy summer, I made the decision to keep Laura's demand for us to leave to myself as we had holidays planned and I was not going to be the one to spoil summer. There was also the element that I had got pretty caught up with watching *Breaking Bad,* which reminded me to live life by my own rules, added to that I had started to draft this book and was in search of a good ending (the old, be careful what you ask for!). There is no doubt that I was a little cuckoo at this point.

The following month as we holidayed in Italy, I received what was likely to be my monthly countdown text which read, *Five months*. I kept the text to myself and quietly put her on block.

Upon returning from our holiday and before Marc returned to the Alps, we had gone to our local supermarket and lo and behold, who did we meet but Clément! We had been packing up our groceries when I spied him walking into the shop. I watched him closely as he came into the shop and observed him as he snatched a look at Marc and me. He stood at the counter as confident as you like when we both walked down to see him. He was wearing his 'I am the king of the castle' face, a self-satisfactory expression that encompassed smiling eyes and a wide grin. He may as well have worn a tee-shirt that said, *C'etait Moi*.

What this man did not know was that Marc was completely unaware of what was going on. He had just enjoyed a fantastic Italian holiday, had his fix of pizza and *Birra Moretti* and was preparing to head back up to the Alps. All was good in Marc's life. It therefore took Clément by surprise when we walked up to him to ask how he was in our usual friendly and casual fashion. When Marc suggested that he call into see him at his shop to collect some things he had stored in a back unit, Clément went into panic mode, and he started to quickly spew out invented excuses as to why he could not meet up. I recall it being something along the lines of a client purchasing one of the most expensive items in his shop, which I guess was thrown in to impress and had not one ounce of truth to it.

At least now I had confirmation of exactly who was behind this stunt. Two can play games and I decided to keep Marc out of this to allow him to focus on making money and creating our future. I was used to living in the land of the crazy and I was starting to understand how their minds worked, which gave me a fighting chance to play their game to my rules...or so I thought.

Fourteen

WTF

Coming from Scotland, I was aware that the clan mentality still existed amongst some families and that in small pockets of Scotland nothing had changed since the days of William Wallace, when knives were hidden in socks for defence or attack. Fiercely loyal to their clan, anyone, and I mean anyone, who had the audacity to say anything even slightly negative about any member of their family is likely to be discussed as follows.

Play

Beware of the Scottish Clan

Act One, Scene One
(*Wee Tam comes home from work in an anxious state.*)

Tam: Da, I just met Willie doon the pub and he heard that Jimmy McDonald said somethin' bad aboot ma maw.

Da: Whit wis it he said, Tam?

Tam: I dinnae remember whit Willie said Jimmy said but it wisnae good. Can you phone your brothers to tell them?

Da: Aye, sure, son, never did like the McDonalds, they are a bad family, and that Jimmy, he is no getting' away with speaking aboot your maw like that.

Act Two, Scene Two
(*Seven uncles, ten nephews, two aunts, two nieces, all tattooed and in their best sports gear, cram into a small sitting room drinking from an assortment of Irn-bru and Special Brew, planning their revenge.*)

The End

As we hurtled our way towards our seventh French Christmas, I thought it time to discuss what had happened with Marc. It was a difficult business keeping this stressful time to myself, and it was a relief almost to share what had happened. Both Laura and Clément had been quiet. I had forgotten that I had placed Laura on block, and I thought that if they still wanted us out, they would have called in to speak with me or at least have telephoned Marc, but nothing had eventuated.

Marc wasn't surprised at the news and immediately got on the phone to Clément to find out what was going on.

"My wife and I, we separate. I cannot live with that woman anymore. We go to get a divorce and she want to go back to our old house. You must get out. Laura, she speak with Abi and she say six months. Why Abi not listen? Laura, she has sent lots of texts to Abi. You must be kind. You must leave our house."

Marc explained that I had chosen to put his wife on block and that we had no plans to move unless we received a letter legally explaining why we were being asked to leave, and dated on the date they were now speaking as opposed to six months previous. A text message asking us to leave had no legality to it, Marc pointed out to Clément.

"My wife, she knows all things legal. I ask her to send a letter, but you must get out."

Within a day or two, we received a letter signed by Laura and backdated to June, indicating her wish to move back into her old house due to their separation. Unlike all the other times that they had split up, I had seen them together both at the shop and in the car on numerous occasions, which confirmed that they had not split up. They simply wanted us to get out.

We had received our second tax document by this stage and in any other normal year we could have gone around searching for another rental, but lockdown was on and off, limiting our movements, and the vaccine had yet to be administered so we were reluctant to move. Beth had decided that she liked being schooled online and we had found an English online school where she planned to start the following September. We were soon to have the freedom to move to the Alps, but January was not a good time in which to move to an area encased in snow.

I chose on this occasion to return the letter to Laura with a note stating that we would move out, but it would not be until the summer as we wished Beth to remain at school to complete her exams.

Now this is where the story of living in Provence hits a crescendo, allowing me to introduce to you an array of people who suddenly flooded unexpectedly into my life. Coming from

Scotland and being aware of clan mentality, I should have known better, but in my defence, I was unaware at this time that Laura's family owned half the village.

The characters continue to include Laura and Clément; their son, Michael; and two local policemen, one a slightly flirtatious man who despite carrying a gun in his holster did not apparently have any authority to deal with illegal activities and the other who made it evident that despite being a policeman, he was not prepared to get involved with the family with whom I was now caught up. Finally, you will be introduced to the family that own an *informatique* shop and will learn that the word *informatique* in these parts can translate directly into English as thieving/illegal/dishonest bastards.

And so it was that when we marched into the following year, one morning, I saw Laura arrive with her son, Michael, and go into their garage situated under our house. They were there for some time, and I knew there was nothing in the garage as I had once taken a sneaky peek as there was no lock on the door. After around thirty minutes, I heard them drive off and when I went down on the lookout for clues, I noticed that they had installed a lock on the door. What were they up to?

Turning on our computers later that morning and it was soon discovered that she had installed something or other below the garage to interfere with the WIFI. A quick text to my brother, who was a tech dude, and he suggested that she may have installed something called a jammer. He questioned if that was likely with us living in Provence, and did we really know people who would do such a thing? Apparently, yes.

As I walked into the police station, there were many men of varying ages sitting around as they all sat back yacking and drinking coffee. As the men looked me up and down, murmuring to each other under their breath, the policeman in charge quickly dismissed the male group to allow me to take a seat.

The officer could see that I was a little shaken up and offered me a glass of water, which I readily accepted as it also gave me time to relax and to construct in my head what I wished to say in French.

I briefly explained the situation and he confirmed that my proprietor was thwarting the law with not providing us with documentation for renting the house (I omitted, of course, to mention that was the only reason we got the house) and he quickly called Clément. He put the call on loudspeaker.

Clément was clearly annoyed at being called and explained to the policeman in no uncertain terms that it was not his house and that him and his wife had separated and with that he gave the policeman Laura's number.

As Laura's number rang out, the policeman left a message to say that if she did indeed have any jammer under the house that she was to remove this with immediate effect and that as a proprietor she was to try to rectify in a peaceful manner our differences.

The officer explained to me that he had no authority as such, and his place in the village was solely to sort out disputes between neighbours and of those, he assured me, as he raised his eyebrows, there were many.

As I left the station, I thanked him for his time, and he assured me that he would open a case file and would note down what had happened should his colleague be on the desk if there was to be a second visit.

To my relief, later that evening, our WIFI was back up and running.

A week or so later and I was sitting in my living room texting my brother and two sisters. We were being particularly juvenile that evening as we were looking out old family snaps and, using an app, we were making them sing. Old relatives who had long since departed were now singing to us and we were bringing our baby photos to life. There was a lot of hilarity as we passed these singing snaps back and fore to each other.

It wasn't long after that upon Marc's return home that I decided to show him the videos, but search as I might, they had all vanished. To my surprise, in their place I found some rather peculiar photos of strange people standing behind cameras to portray, I presume, that I was being spied upon. These were subtle hints that on reflection were placed on my phone to scare me, I suppose, but it was too subtle, and without wanting to come across as going insane, I rationally put them down to pictures being sent and stored from WhatsApp because it was a time when WhatsApp was the app that allowed us to get through lockdown and was viewed and used when sober and when not so.

There was, however, my alarm that, despite me setting it, was going off some mornings and not others. I put this down to having an old iPhone. I noticed a reduction in messages from my sisters, which was unusual as they texted me most days, and then there was the evening that I was watching France play Scotland in rugby. Just as Scotland were about to score their final try that would win the match, our Orange box knocked off. By the time I managed to get it up and working again, the match had ended and I had missed the winning try.

They must have thought by this stage that I was on drugs because I continued to live as before; working, headphones on, singing and a-dancing and generally just enjoying my life, so I gather the tribe decided to step it up a notch.

One morning after I had dropped Beth at the *lycée* and returned home, I finished my breakfast, opened my MacBook to get to work and noticed that I had a guest user. My desktop had been rearranged. As I looked up to check my VPN, I noticed that it was off, so I checked my network connection and switched my VPN back on. I watched as it was switched off, and each time I put it on, someone, I realised, was switching it off. I reached down and knocked off the WIFI. WTF.

It was then that it occurred, or should I say, finally dawned on me, that all the little oddities that had been happening were real and not figments of my imagination caused by my newfound suspicious nature. They were in my telephone and had been for some time.

I recalled the feeling of being watched, right back to when we moved into the house. It was such an overwhelming feeling that I had searched every nook and cranny of the house in search of listening devices or cameras, but I had failed to find anything. I never considered for one moment that anyone would hack into my telephone, but now as I looked at my iPhone, I knew well, as the French might say, that someone was in it and possibly had been for longer than I wished to imagine.

Mind games, I was being caught up in them. Nothing glaringly obvious, just a drip, drip, drip.

I was a very trusting person up until I arrived in Provence.

The jammer, it seemed, had been replaced by something else, something more sinister. Now they had my full attention.

I reflected on the past few weeks and in particular an evening that Beth and I had returned home from the Alps as Marc had asked if we wouldn't mind coming up last minute to help with some painting. My birthday was coming up and I knew that gifts were waiting for me in my letterbox, as I had texts from the couriers to confirm this was the case. When I arrived home and opened my letterbox, it was surprisingly empty and it was then that I heard my name being shouted, and as I looked in the direction of the voice, I could see see my little plump neighbour, who was waving her hands about as she tried to explain something that looked to be fairly serious. She could see from my response, or lack of it, that I had not a clue as to what she was talking about, so she turned around and came down the stairs, running across the road to where I was standing.

Keeping in mind that COVID was still doing the rounds and we were supposed to be keeping our distance from each other, she ran right across the road and standing about 5 cm from my face, she began to explain that she had watched the same vehicle pull up on three separate occasions to go into my letterbox. She held up three fingers, pointed to a car and then to my letterbox to ensure that I could understand her. When I asked if she knew the people, she looked at me weirdly and slowly nodded her head before running back to her house. Whoever was thieving must have had access to my phone as I received a text each time a delivery was expected, or if I was not at home when a parcel was being dropped off.

With the news that my birthday presents had been taken, it is fair to say that I was rather disappointed, and that Beth was angry as she had selected something online that she was very excited about me opening. We had chosen to mope, sitting in the kitchen drinking our hot chocolate, when the doorbell rang, and there she was again, my small plump neighbour, this time holding out a paper plate on which were laid two slices of homemade mascarpone cake. It was a kind gesture but what concerned me was the almost petrified look on her face.

I was now joining all the dots and started to recall some strange texts from Clément where he had told me:

I have spoken with my computer friend and I now have the same phone as you.

    I have spoken with my computer friend and I have bought the same MacBook as you.

Just like the late and hideous Jimmy Savile – "*My case is coming up next Thursday*" – the clues were there, but just like stinky old Jimmy, we overlooked them because we chose to laugh at this crazy character who had entered our lives feigning friendship.

The weirdness of events escalated and one afternoon I received an email from Beth's school that simply stated, *You have well received my letter.* It was clearly not from Beth's school. What letter? I ran down to the letter box to find an official letter which upon opening was from my beloved landlady, Laura. The letter stated that she wished to have workmen come into the house to complete work prior to her moving back into her old family home. She looked to be a whizz with computers.

I will now introduce you to a family who owned a shop that repaired computers, referred to in France as *un magasin d'informatique.* Their shop was situated in the village next to mine. An *informatique* shop did reside in my own village but during the initial lockdown I had called in to buy a charger, and as she did not have one, I placed an order which she assured me would arrive within the week but as it was lockdown it may take longer. Fair enough. Over the next four weeks, I called in over six times and on each occasion she told me that it had yet to arrive. I had gone ahead and purchased one elsewhere but as I had paid for this one, I wanted to collect it. I waited another three weeks and called back in, feeling sure by this stage it would have arrived. She looked at me like she had never clapped eyes on me before in her life and asked if I had a receipt. I replied that she had not given me one, but as this was my seventh visit to her shop, did she not remember me? She shook her head and said that she had never seen me before and that if she had not given me a receipt then she had never taken my money. The second WTF of this chapter.

Therefore, I opted to avoid my village *informatique* shop, who were clearly useless, and opted instead to go to an *informatique* shop in the next village that I had visited previously when Beth had an issue with the sound on her MacBook. On this visit, I had entered the shop and was met by a man I presumed to be the owner. He was around 6ft in height, dark haired and was wearing glasses. He was neither attractive nor unattractive, just a plain-looking man devoid of any friendliness, which I found unusual as owners always try to be welcoming. I found him very straight to the point, and he asked that he keep Beth's MacBook over the evening to allow him to repair the sound and for me to call back the next day. I recall when entering the shop that he had a back office as I remember seeing a woman around his own age, slightly plump with her hair in some bizarre bunches-type style, that I presumed to be his wife, coming out of the office, standing and staring at me in the same manner as Laura would stare at a woman that she felt might wish to whisk her husband away. I had to some extent become used to this bizarre coupling in Provence but nonetheless I found it a little unnerving. It is fair to say that when I decided to go to the shop on the second occasion, with so much on my mind, I had forgotten about this weird couple that resided within.

So that afternoon, being unsure as to what was happening, and questioning whether Laura and Clément would really sink so low as to hack into my devices, I marched in with both my own MacBook and Beth's, just to ask them to check if there were any viruses contained in either and for them to explain to me how someone had gotten into our computers. At this stage, having only ever used my computer for work, I had no clue whatsoever as to how someone could have accessed them and how I was to stop this from happening.

I immediately recognised the owner as I walked into the shop and in normal circumstances, he should have remembered me too and welcomed me as I entered but instead, he just stood there staring at me in some sort of trance almost. I noticed that when I started to speak to explain what was happening, his wife, sporting a new but still as bizarre as the last hairdo, came venturing again out of the back office. There was no friendly acknowledgement from her either and like her husband, she opted to stand behind the back counter and stare. My ability to speak French becomes vastly reduced when I am stressed, and it took me all my time and effort to construct a sentence. I noticed that as I continued and gained the inner strength to mention that this might all be the doing of my proprietor, his look became even more intense. With that, a boy ventured out of the office behind the front counter, a boy in his mid-twenties, who I presumed to be their son. As I bumbled on with my take on events, they chose to listen to me in eerie silence. At that point, because of the seriousness of being hacked by my landlady, I had naively assumed that they were staring at me out of shock for what had happened. When the owner finally spoke, he said that he doubted my landlady would have done such a thing but if I was to leave my laptops, he would run checks through them. He was to call me when they were ready.

It took several days for me to receive a call. When I entered the shop, which was now my third visit, I was met with the same lack of friendliness as before but this time the owner was wearing a very rigid and serious expression.

"You have picked up a virus from having been on the dark web." He literally threw this statement at me as I entered without even having the opportunity to make it to the counter. I nearly choked on the small amount of saliva that was circulating in my mouth.

"The what?" I asked. "What are you speaking of?"

At that, the younger man came out of the office behind the front counter and explained to me that I had been surfing the dark web and that it was likely that this was the reason why I now had problems with both my laptops and my telephone. I had mentioned my telephone on the previous visit. I knew well the existence of the dark web, but if my life had depended upon it, I had no clue as to how to access it. I did know that it was somewhere that would allow me to hire a hitman, and I was starting to believe that one was necessary. The owner assured me that he had deleted anything relating to the dark web and had run various virus checkers through our devices.

"Is everything okay now?" I asked before reluctantly producing my card.

"Oh yes," he replied. "Everything is fine. There are no viruses on either of your devices."

With that remark, he printed out the invoice relating to Beth's laptop and circled the word *nothing* as he confirmed for the second time that there were no viruses to be found on this laptop. The cost was 65€. I paid for this invoice and then he took my card again and put my payment through. He handed me my receipt for 200.01€ (the 1 was clearly to have a laugh at my expense) and I noticed this time that he did not produce an invoice for my laptop. He was extraordinarily rude and abrupt and that set me to wondering.

After a brief walk around the local supermarket to clear my mind, I managed to get my head together and walked back in, this time prepared for a confrontation.

On this instance, the owner did not appear to be present, and it was the younger man that came out of his office to see me. Instead of opting to speak, I put my phone in front of him and handed him a written note that said, *Do you know my proprietor?* and as he read it, he looked at where I had placed my mobile phone directly in front of him on the counter, reached out and tossed it to the far side of the long counter, and as he returned to look at me, he had a terrified expression and raising his eyebrows, he nodded slowly to indicate that my proprietor was indeed in my telephone. "Sorry," he quietly muttered. I did feel with the look on his face that he was in fact sorry, but if he was working for his parents, what options were there? None. He had also just admitted to being the one who had in fact accessed all our devices. His father was clearly the computer friend Clément had mentioned on several occasions. Drip.

You are probably tired just reading this shit but, believe me, it was far more tiresome and stressful living it!

Confirmation then that either Laura or Clément was in my phone and had been for some time. They also had access to Beth's. I thought back to an afternoon when Marc had taken Clément for lunch and Clément had suggested going to an Asian restaurant quite far out of town. Beth and I had stumbled upon this restaurant the week previous. Was this a coincidence or had he been tracking me? It would have been a hell of a coincidence considering he seldom left his leaf, and when he did, we had never heard him talk about eating Asian food; he was a traditional restaurant kind of man. Another drip…I guess.

When I returned home and switched on my laptop, I found myself unable to access any of my files, and the realisation that I had just paid 200.01€ for the privilege was disheartening to say the least. Yet another *arnaque*. I had been truly and utterly framed and I bet they could not believe their luck when this naïve Scottish girl turned up at their shop and the opportunity arose to make more money. I was clearly well out of my league.

A second visit to the police station was due. When I entered on this occasion, I was met by a different officer. I had chosen to leave my phone, which was now a listening device, at home, but I did take my MacBook to show that my computer had been hacked and as I explained the admittance of the *informatique* shop, his face clouded over. He had no idea what I was talking about.

"Can you not look on your computer, as your colleague assured me that he had logged my complaint?" I asked in French.

With that, he smiled, shook his head and, leaning back on his chair, asked me what I wished for him to do. My complaint had clearly not been logged.

On my insistence that he phone Laura, he went ahead and called her and as they spoke, I realised that they knew each other. I listened as they chatted about people in the village and laughed at my inability to speak good French. When they had finished laughing and catching up, he came off the phone, twirled his chair around, sat up and leant forward in my direction.

"Why are you living in this house?" he asked in French. "Get out."

I explained in my naïve manner that what they were doing was illegal. I watched as he shook his head slowly and said to me in English:

"That is true, yes, but I give you this advice. I know well this family, and you must get out."

His demeanour was serious and that was enough for me. I had listened in to their conversation and it was evident that they viewed me as an outsider and that he was siding with one of his own.

I am going to venture off for a moment as I recall an evening when Marc, Beth and I had gone out for dinner at a restaurant in the next village and stumbled upon an end-of-summer fête. I was wearing a pair of high-heeled sandals which were comfortable enough, but that evening, after leaving the restaurant, we ended up joining a procession that took us almost a mile outside the village to a field where fireworks were to be set off. All the village looked to be in the procession, and we were all following men dressed as miners who were dragging behind them large trolleys containing giant speakers that were blasting out ominous-sounding music, like what you might hear if you were to watch an Alfred Hitchcock movie. Was a bit wacky. Once the fireworks had finished and we were all walking back to the village, I overheard an English father and his daughter speaking as they walked behind me.

"You see the ridiculous shoes the lady in front is wearing, how did she think these were practical for this evening? They look so uncomfortable."

I laughed when I heard this as the father had obviously assumed with speaking so loudly that I was French and could not understand what he was saying, so I turned around and responded.

"For your information, Monsieur Englishman, my sandals are extremely comfortable."

His face, and that of his daughter, was a picture.

Back to the police station.

I got up to leave, politely thanked this man for whatever I was to thank him for, which amounted to nothing really, and walked back to my car.

I had wondered when we had arrived in Provence why there was a necessity for an *informatique* shop in each small village and now I had my answer.

I couldn't use my internet as they were watching my every move, but I did know where a removal company was located, and the following morning, I called in to arrange for our belongings to be uplifted on the first available date.

I called Marc to explain the situation and he arranged to come home to help me pack.

We were going to be leaving this crazy ass place and as much as we had all enjoyed such great times in this house, particularly when family came over to visit, it was dawning on us that our Provence adventure was coming to a conclusion and it was time for us all to be together, this time in the French Alps.

I was concerned about Beth as the news that they had access to her computer and telephone was overwhelming for her. I wanted her to leave this situation as quickly as possible. We had promised her a new laptop and mobile phone and she decided that these were not to be Apple products. They had accessed our devices easily because they were all linked. We were not going to make the same mistake again, plus we were going to have to learn to be more computer savvy.

The removal company were busy so it was going to take another two weeks before we could leave. This gave Marc time to contact a client who had approached him to renovate a large chalet that he rented out over the winter months to ask if they would consider renting their chalet to us over the spring, summer and autumn months of that year. To our delight an agreement was reached, and Beth and I could now relax knowing that we were going to live in an equally astounding setting.

Marc and I opened a few bottles of fizz that week to celebrate and to reflect on the good times that we had enjoyed whilst living in Provence. Provence, all things considered, had been an incredible place to stay. We had finally experienced what it felt like to have four distinct seasons that ran like clockwork. With each season, our surroundings would undergo significant changes that we would relish often choosing to stop on the way to the supermarket, picture postcard moments for example, when poppies arrived in the springtime, turning plain fields and grass verges into an unforgettable scene. Of course, Provence would not be Provence without its fields of sunflowers and lavender and then there are the vines. In the winter months, Beth, when she first arrived in Provence, would be sure to tell us that the vines had died and sure enough as they were pruned in the early winter months, it was hard to imagine that these would ever blossom again, but sure enough as spring kicked in, it was a joy to see these wrinkled stems slowly coming to life and with each trip past we would witness the vines growing until finally we would spy the grapes. Our village was one that lived and breathed wine and when harvest time came upon us, we would know as tractors drove past our house in the early hours of the morning and as the day went by, we would see them return with large trailers filled to the brim with dark purple grapes, often spilling over the sides.

It was these treasured moments that despite all the shenanigans made our stay in Provence unforgettable. It was also becoming unforgettable now for reasons we had not envisaged.

Us leaving, was a good opportunity for a clear out, as Marc was continually bringing things down with him on each trip south, and the house, garden and garage had become cluttered.

With Marc having completed his spring cleaning, we decided that it was the right time for Marc to take Beth with him to start the new adventure early. They packed up the van until bursting point and squashing the door closed and with arms stretched out of the window to wave, they sped off.

My once happy home had turned into one big listening device. I had no intention of knocking my phone off and with the continued lockdown I had no opportunity to purchase another telephone. It wasn't just my phone they had control of, they had also been deleting my emails which explained why I was not receiving emails from my clients. With a call to a colleague, they were able to change passwords and to email my clients on my behalf to explain the situation. They were unable to stop phone calls, but they were deleting all my messages that were being sent to me on my mobile.

With Marc and Beth having left, they would know for sure that we were packed up and they would have seen my text to the removal company to confirm that we were leaving their house, surely now they would leave us alone? I tried to see the funny side of it all and took to speaking in the phone to ask how they both were, throwing in a few derogatory remarks. I know they had heard them, because not long after my insult, which was as best as I could come up with as I thought how the French may insult each other, my iTunes account was accessed, and my playlist was deleted. I now had a week to get through with a few Madonna albums and a few Metallica tracks. It was going to be a long week.

I stumbled my way though that week on a rollercoaster of emotions. I was sad to be leaving Provence as I adored the laid-back lifestyle that I had adapted to. I had certainly had enough of the family we had become embroiled with and with recent events it was clear that no matter how I felt that I was fitting in, I would always be seen as a tourist in the eyes of those around me. I was however happy that we had chosen to move to France and not

Italy, as at this stage of me refusing to leave the house, it was likely that my body may now have been buried under one of the back terraces.

As I sat having my meal and a glass of wine in the evenings after spending the day painting the shutters and jet washing the terraces, I reflected on our journey so far. We had arrived in France knowing exactly what we desired. We got the old traditional house with pool, we each wound down from our fast-paced lives and made the most of the blue-sky days. Meals, in particular, lunches were eaten outside for much of the year and in the winter evenings with a fire pit, we would sit enjoying a few beers under the night sky. It was never a hardship when family visited and they wished to go wine tasting, it was just a case of dwindling it down to certain ones, as there were so many vineyards on our doorstep, to choose from.

Learning to make a reservation prior to arriving at our local restaurants was invaluable advice as we were met by each proprietor with a handshake and a warm welcome as opposed to being quizzed. Stripping down to a bikini and reading a book on our favored beach on a hot summer's day was blissful. With it choosing to rain overnight, my umbrella had little use. So many good times and so much to be thankful for. As for the crazy family, I chose to put this down to the universe working in mysterious ways. Where would we have lived if we had not met them?

The week seemed to drag in, and it was with great joy and utter relief when I got to the end of it. I wasn't sure what else to expect from Laura, as if she had no hesitation in damaging my neighbor's car, she would have no hesitation in damaging mine. I had already noticed a small scratch down the side of my passenger door, so to be on the safe side I had put my car in my now de-cluttered garage.

That evening I set my alarm although I had a feeling that someone was going to ensure that it did not go off. As a backup I phoned Marc to ask him to call me in the morning just to be sure although I had a feeling that I would not receive his call.

My internal clock woke me up on the dot, which was just as well as my alarm clearly had been knocked off and I received no telephone call from Marc. I had left my telephone the previous evening in the kitchen because I had thought a few days previously that I had heard someone speak through my phone when I was out painting the shutters. Sure enough, that morning my phone spoke to me in a female voice, and in English, it said, "We had to think of some way to get you out of the house."

I had never lived through anything so crazy in my life. It was utterly ridiculous.

Was what was happening to me now, normal around these parts? I was on a quest to find out and so in between my visits to the *Informatique* shop and the Police station, minus my mobile, I paid a visit to my bank manager. I was eager to change passwords to my online bank as with previous access to my laptop they would have been able to access our accounts. Our bank manager was a quiet and respectful man in his mid-thirties. As I talked him through recent events he responded, "unfortunately that mentality does exist in these parts." And when I recounted what had happened with the owner of the *informatique* shop, he responded, "These companies are not all like that, there are some that are honest." I happened that week to bump into a British friend of mine at the supermarket and when she heard my story she laughed "Abi, that does not surprise me in the least, the French are crazy, truly crazy."

The greatest sight that week was not the poppy fields, as beautiful as they were, the most glorious sight was the removal van pulling up outside of my house. I could have hugged these guys.

Once packed up, there was the matter of handing over keys. I had considered leaving them with the local *mairie* but when I arrived at their office, it was closed. Was I strong enough and was I brave enough to do what I wanted to do?

Just about, and so it was that I quickly scribbled a letter and putting both the letter and the keys into an envelope, I said my goodbyes, to what we had considered home for a short period of time at least, and getting in my car, drove off to visit the two weirdest people I had ever met in my life. It was time to give them a surprise visit.

As I drove down their long driveway, I could see Clément sitting under his porch area, smoking. The trees lining his driveway obviously blocked my car from view and he must have thought it was one of his children visiting, so it would have been a shock for him to see me as I parked my car and opened my door, slowly getting out and walking over to where he had been sitting.

I say *had been sitting*, because when he saw me pull up, he frantically leapt out of his seat and bolted into the kitchen. The kitchen door had been open, and I saw Laura with cloth in hand, cleaning down the worktops.

"Abi, she is here," I heard him shout as he bolted in to hide behind the apron strings of his replacement mother.

"Abi, she is here?" I heard her repeat in panic.

I was in all honesty expecting a confrontation, but no, these two sad individuals remained hiding in their kitchen as I walked slowly down to their porch table and threw down the envelope containing their keys and the letter, slowly walking back to my car before driving off. 'A lion in a cage'. I smiled as I thought of his description of himself as this was the most cowardly lion I had ever come across since watching *The Wizard of Oz*.

I reflected on the letter that Marc and I had agreed upon before he had left for the Alps. We were unsure if they were intentionally looking to create problems for us as a family or if their own personal inability to function as a partnership was solely behind this, so we intended to keep things normal at our end. We also felt that with their competitive and jealous nature, Marc trading in his old transit for a far newer model prior to lockdown would not have helped matters. So, our letter that I dropped off that day, read very much like this, allowing for translation from French into English for easy reading.

Dear Clément and Laura,

Thank you so much for allowing us to rent your beautiful home. It was so kind of you both.

As promised, we have painted the house and have left it in a far better condition than when we received it. We left you the Siemens oven that we had installed and the kitchen table that Marc made to enhance the look of your kitchen. All the windows and shutters have been painted and the terraces jet washed. We hope your new tenants will enjoy your house as much as we did.

We wish you all a very happy life.

With much love,

Marc, Abi & Beth

Xxx

As I made my way up and out of their driveway, I selected an old favourite, *Nothing Else Matters* by Metallica, a song in truth that collectively we had all listened to many times that week, and with such a limited playlist I did not have anything that exceeded it in terms of attitude. So, lowering my windows, I cranked it up and as I made my way out of Provence, I felt as free as a bird. I imagined myself flying up to the Alps, leaving behind people who in my mind were all stuck in cages, squabbling and fighting and gossiping being their driving forces.

Le prédateur et sa femme jalouse, what a joyous union!

I was fueled by adrenalin and I guessed at this stage it was likely to be on the low side and about to hit empty. Would they be satisfied now that we had left, I wondered, or was this a personal vendetta? Only time would tell. I had several hours drive ahead of me, so I switched on the radio tuning into the local stations as I sung my way up to the Alps. As I wound my way up passing signs that said *Heaven this way*, I finally reached the signpost that led me to our new home.

Our second adventure was about to commence.

Acknowledgements

Opting to up sticks and leave the country in which you were born is not always easy for family and friends, especially when they themselves enjoy living in the country you have turned your back on. We therefore feel hugely privileged to belong to families who have allowed us to be free. Together they have offered us emotional, and at times, financial help, to overcome various obstacles as we found our feet in this beautiful yet challenging country. Having the freedom to live is one that we had previously taken for granted.

First and foremost, my heartfelt thanks go to Marc. Your sacrifice to move away from the part of France that you fell in love with to ensure that your income gave us all a chance to enjoy not just a good life but a great one, will forever be appreciated. Never did you put pressure on me to leave Provence and instead you supported the freedom attached to the *oiseau* that you chose to marry. I know well that your friends at times thought Beth and I were figments of your imagination. I recall your words "When I choose my next wife, I will make sure her dream is to have a sandpit and a Peugeot." Whilst these words continue to make me laugh, you nonetheless ran with me on my quest to attain my childhood dream. So many good times. Who can forget Suzie Sandblaster? You are a fantastic companion as we travel together through this crazy journey called life. I love you heaps.

To our beautiful Beth. For your long-lasting patience as we gathered our strength and our finances together to finally take the leap of faith to move to France. Perhaps we asked too much of you, on reflection, with the adjustments that you have had to make in your young life. Seldom did you complain as you trundled off to school each day to learn your lessons in a language, that for the most part, you were endeavouring to pick up as you went along. I am extremely grateful to you for your input for this book, all the memes, quotes and YouTube videos that you pass to me, particularly, the swimming pool full of dogs that you sent with the message 'A *clear representation of our time in Provence.*' You have added such joy to our lives. *Je t'adore ma chérie.*

To Marc's parents. Thank you for supporting our move and for never putting any pressure on us to settle in New Zealand. We thank you as a family for helping us out financially when Marc had to find a way to travel in snowy conditions and needed an alternative mode of transport.

To my sister Cherry. A huge thank you for choosing to spend your summer holidays with us. Great memories! You understood well, the various pickles we found ourselves in, and when things took an unexpected turn in our final months, you were on stand-by, purchasing new mobiles and laptops that allowed us to quickly get ourselves back on track when we arrived in the Alps. Thank you also for being our guarantor, providing us with the backing we needed when renting in the Alps, as we await the completion of our renovation project. Finally, a massive thank you for taking an interest in this book, making time in your busy work schedule to edit my first draft, as you showed me how best to improve my scribblings. Your positivity and encouragement allowed me to finally get this book finished.

To my brother Jey, for selecting as a birthday gift, *The World My Wilderness* by Rose Macaulay. Her words helped me to steer this book in the right direction. Thank you also for the thoughtfulness of giving Marc the *Dictionary of French Building Terms*.

To my beautiful and dependable friend Elizabeth. Thank you for reading my first draft, which was dreadful (and some may well say that it still is). You loyally ploughed your way through it, nonetheless, remaining positive on my initial efforts.

To my beautiful father, wherever you may be. I miss you and thank you from the bottom of my heart for finding the strength to come out to spend time with us in Provence on three separate occasions. I hope that you have found your darling Elizabeth and are making up for lost time. I miss you both very much and feel sure we will all meet again...

To my Welsh family. Thank you for listening to me prattling on about my ridiculous life. You guys' rock.

To Iain. Thank you for reading through my final draft and for your valued comments.

To our accountant here in France who was more than obliging as he came to our home to set us up in the French system, without asking for any fee. Your advice to take on any type of work, just to cover the bills until we were able to find more suitable employment, was valuable advice as was your encouragement as you recalled to us your own personal account of your initial hardships and the level of determination required in order to make it in France. We hope that your faith in us is paying off.

To Scott Gibson at *elegantW3*, thank you for your support during *hacking-gate*, for re-setting passwords for all our business websites, and email accounts, and for reaching out to my clients to explain the bizarre situation I had found myself in. Thank you also for all your website creations over the years. Always reliable. Always professional.

To Marc Mechan at *Red Axe Design*. When you presented me with your initial sketches, it was as if you had pulled them straight out of my brain. You nailed it, and I am delighted with your work. Thank you so much.

To all the team at Troubador, thank you for your patience and your professionalism.

And finally, a huge thank you to Scott Witham at *Traffic Design*, for designing my book cover. Always ready to run with my crazy notions and ideas. Always dependable. Always exceeding expectations.

'A bird should always have the freedom
to fly high into the sky.'

About the Author

À votre santé!